For the
Love of Language

POETRY FOR EVERY LEARNER

For the
Love of Language

POETRY FOR EVERY LEARNER

NANCY LEE CECIL

Peguis Publishers
Winnipeg • Manitoba • Canada

Printed and bound in Canada by Hignell Printing Limited

94 95 96 97 98   5 4 3 2 1

Canadian Cataloguing in Publication Data

Cecil, Nancy Lee

For the love of language: poetry for every learner

Includes bibliographical references.
ISBN 1-895411-61-0

1. Poetry – Study and teaching (Elementary).
2. Creative writing (Elementary education).   3. Language arts (Elementary).   I. Title.

LB1576.C4   1994   372.6'23   C93-098190-1

Book and Cover Design: Laura Ayers
Cover Illustration: Ken Stampnick
Text illustrations: Pamela Dixon

Peguis Publishers Ltd.
520 Hargrave Street
Winnipeg, MB
Canada R3A 0X8

For Dr. Harold Roeder, who first inspired me.

Contents

Part II: Intermediate Scaffolds

Acknowledgments

Heartfelt thanks go to the teachers and preservice teachers in the San Juan School District who tried out many poem ideas; to the children who wrote the poems and allowed me to publish them; to Annalee Greenberg, whose enthusiasm for the project and thoughtful feedback assisted me enormously; to my husband Gary for his infinite patience and support; to my lovely daughter, Chrissy, who showed me so clearly that every child is a poet.

I Introduction

The children of the nineties bring a rich mix of experiential, ethnic, linguistic, religious, and cultural backgrounds to the schoolhouse door—differences whose nuances must be recognized, appreciated, and accommodated for any instructional program to be successful. In California, for example, over half the elementary school-age children are Hispanic, African American, or Asian. One child in six was born in another country. Children from over eighty language groups who are just learning English make up 29 percent of those students entering kindergarten (California Department of Education 1992). Additionally, in this state as in many other states and provinces of North America, many children have sad stories to tell: by some estimates, as many as 85 percent of all children in our schools can in some way be classified as "children of trauma" by virtue of broken homes, abuse, neglect, poverty, or drug or alcohol abuse in their homes (Middleton-Moz 1989). Children with such problems are found, in varying degrees, all over the United States and Canada. In far too many schools it appears to be "business as usual," as teachers continue to teach much as they have always taught. For example, teachers are still generating writing topics from their own culture and values, to which children must respond with a teacher-specified number of words ("Write 500 words on what you did on your summer vacation"), and children are still being asked to fill in blanks in voluminous workbook pages, supposedly developing a series of isolated reading and writing skills for which they can see no real purpose. Many teachers,

1

however, are concerned about these problems. Yet they are unsure of how to cope with the changing curricular needs of today's child. Poetry may well be a significant component of the needed curricular reform for these children.

Why Poetry?

All children are natural poets; poetry is a universal language that can offer children a viable outlet for confusing feelings that they long to express and make sense of. Moreover, poetry reaches to the heart, not the head, of the learner, in a whimsical language that appeals to children. Poetry allows children to speak and write freely in their own special language rather than the more formal language of the other modes of discourse, with all of their rigid conventions. When introduced in the manner described in this book, poetry writing becomes not a laborious task of constructing a composition about an unknown topic, but an enjoyable way to play with language in response to personal thoughts, feelings, and observations. John Dewey maintained that all learning must emanate from the interest of the learner; poetry, correctly introduced, truly capitalizes on the learner's own interests, experiences, and ideas.

Making Poetry Work

Poetry must be made accessible to *all* children—regardless of primary language and ability level. Unfortunately, this is often not the case (Denman 1988). Additionally, studies as to how children are exposed to poetry at school, if at all, suggest that most teachers use only that poetry included in basal series that the children read in class, or dutifully read the stilted poems found in literature anthologies, hoping to inspire children to "love" poetry (Shapiro 1990). Furthermore, as these selections lack the extensive lesson-planning guidance usually provided for the basal stories, the poems are usually quickly read aloud to the children by the teacher, skipped over entirely, or assigned for the children to memorize and recite in singsong fashion. Thus begins and ends the poetry program in most elementary schools.

To engage the reluctant and the fearful with poetry—teachers and children alike—it may first be necessary to redefine poetry. Too often we think of poetry as a rather profound, highly original piece of writing with a carefully metered rhyme scheme. By broadening what we mean by this all-too-esoteric term, we expand it to encompass all that anyone could think or imagine—in any language—and we increase the possibilities that children will enjoy poetry and want to create their own poems.

Redefining Poetry

A poem is
- a mirror in which the poet sees himself or herself
- a stream of consciousness woven together from a million half-remembered memories
- a song in which the poet furnishes his or her own tune
- a riddle asked by the poet who isn't there to tell the answer, doesn't know the answer, or doesn't care about the answer
- the poet's most intimate thoughts masqueraded, which only those who care about him or her recognize
- a garden of words that can be planted in neat rows, but then again, can grow wild and free
- a thought, an experience, a reflection, a mood, a color, an observation, an idea, a picture, or a question set in a design of words

In this book, you will find examples of poetry written by children that are all these things and more. By learning to use the literacy scaffolds provided, your students will experience language and poetry in fresh and empowering ways.

Sharing Poetry With Children

When children have internalized the broad spectrum of what poetry can be, they are much more willing to listen to poems, "letting them mean," according to their own culture, experiences, and facility with language. To further underscore the infinite possibilities of what poetry can be, you can share a wide variety of genres with your students, including humorous poems, thoughtful poems, alliterative odes, rhymed verse, as well as free verse. Formats as diverse as rap songs, limericks, haiku, and jumping-rope chants can be shared with and enjoyed by children. Moreover, a wide variety of poets could be offered to children including the "great masters" such as Robert Frost, William Blake, and Robert Louis Stevenson, and contemporary favorites such as Jack Prelutsky and Shel Silverstein. The works of children from current and previous classes should also be read frequently.

In this book, using literacy scaffolds, you will explore how to guide children to write their own poetry. But first there is much you can do that will make poetry joyful and non-threatening and transform the classroom into an ideal environment to foster the enjoyment of poetry.

Launching a Poetry Program

To launch a poetry program, select a variety of poetry books and anthologies and have them accessible for browsing and free reading times. Read favorites into a tape recorder to create a poetry listening center where children can listen and follow along or record the poems *they* like best. Collect poems in a poetry file so that at any spare moment during the day an ode or limerick can be read spontaneously (Hoskisson & Tompkins 1987). Finally, encourage poetry reading via a continuing game of Poem in My Pocket, in which children are constantly on the lookout for a poem that especially pleases them. At recess or during special times of the day, classmates, teachers, or guests in the class may ask any child, "What poem is in your pocket?" The child then reads his or her poem or asks the other person to do so.

Certain poems lend themselves to being shared chorally, providing an important yet non-threatening vehicle for group participation. By sharing poems chorally, children learn to feel the basic rhythm of the poem without feeling frustrated when they cannot immediately decode every word.

Poems can be arranged for choral reading using the following variations (Stewig 1981):

- *Echoic:* One child is selected to read the entire poem. The child, designated "the leader," reads each line; then the remaining children repeat, or "echo," it.

- *Refrain:* In poems with repetitive refrains, a leader is chosen to read the main portion of the poem while the rest of the class chants the refrain or chorus.

- *Antiphonal:* For poems with distinct sections, the class is divided into two groups. Each group is assigned one section of the poem to read.

- *Cumulative:* With poems that build in intensity, voices are added with each succeeding line. One student or group starts with the first line or stanza, and a new student or group is added as each line or stanza is read, causing a heightened intensity created by the effect of the cumulative voices.

Some other ways to share poetry follow (Cecil 1993):

- Have children act out a favorite poem, such as Robert Frost's *Stopping by Woods on a Snowy Evening.* Write the poem on the chalkboard or overhead and read aloud; then have the children gather into small groups to discuss what the poem says to them. Finally, have each group act out its impression of the poem for the rest of the class. Children may later want to discuss the groups' contrasting interpretations.
- To provide an active dimension to poetry, poems may be disassembled and then reassembled. Share a poem aloud with the children, then place the lines of the poem on separate strips of tagboard and distribute to groups of children. Then have each group reassemble the poem in front of the class and recite the lines orally.
- Read poems to the class that connote specific moods, then add music and/or sound effects to augment the particular feelings evoked by the poem. For example, you might play a xylophone or water-filled glasses while reading Edgar Allan Poe's *The Bells.* Similarly, a reading of Longfellow's *Song of Hiawatha* might be accompanied by actual drumbeats.

Finally, one of the major concerns you may have is how to fit a poetry program into an already overcrowded curriculum. Writing and sharing poetry with children need not take away from other curricular demands. Poetry, as it is broadly conceived in this text, may be undertaken in language-arts time as it naturally incorporates the discrete areas of reading, writing, listening, and speaking. Moreover, many of the literacy scaffolds presented in this book lend themselves for use as written responses to content area subjects. For example, Two Worders (page 54) could be used as a culminating activity for a unit on whales; Fifteen Words poems (page 80) could easily reinforce a set of readings about the Gaspé Peninsula; whereas Definitions poems (page 40) could be used to underscore conceptual understandings about issues as varied as prejudice, pollution, poverty, or peace.

Using Literacy Scaffolds

For children, especially those who are at risk academically, to begin to see poetry as an exciting and powerful avenue through which they can begin to experiment with their own perceptions and ideas, they must be given additional support with the structure, which can be so frightening as to be overwhelming. Literacy scaffolds, which are simply temporary writing frameworks or models for writing, enable these children to achieve success with poetry. With a structure provided, children can formulate their ideas in ways that might be difficult, if not impossible, without the framework. Literacy scaffolds provide easy-to-follow patterns, or "formulas," for writing poems so that children can focus on their ideas rather than on the mechanics of the poem. Scaffolds can be offered as an option so that children with greater ability and more proficiency in the English language are not held back by their use. All children can use the framework as is, adapt it for their own purposes, or discard it entirely in favor of their own creative agenda.

The literacy scaffold allows children who use it to imitate, to a greater or lesser degree, an existing model, such as the following:

Bees
Bees are buzzy,
Bees are bright.
   Boisterous, belligerent,
   Bothersome, bad.
   Bashful, beautiful,
   Bewildering, bold.
Bees are bright,
Bees are buzzy.

— Nancy Lee Cecil

After chorally reading *Bees*, children are guided to see the pattern (the "scaffold") of describing words (adjectives) used, to notice that each describing word begins with the same sound, and that the last two sentences (the ending couplet) and the beginning two sentences (the beginning couplet) are mirror images of one another. Subsequently, children are asked to think of a favorite animal or object (noun) that the group would like to write a poem about. When the subject has been agreed upon, as a group they brainstorm phrases that might appropriately fit the subject. All words used to describe must, of course, begin with the initial letter of the subject. The dictionary is fair game, and the children are invited to use words from other languages (Cecil & Lauritzen 1994). One class, using the preceding literacy scaffold, created this poem:

Cats

Cats are cute,
Cats are chula (*the Spanish word for "cute"*).
Careful, caring,
Cautious, climbing.
Comforting, cagey,
Confusing, costly.
Cats are chula,
Cats are cute.

— *Mrs. Bertha Schmidt's fifth-grade class*

Because all children in the class had the experience of participating in the creation of the group poem, they were then ready and eager to formulate their own individual poems by imitating the structure of the *Cats* and *Bees* poems, yet incorporating their own ideas and languages. An alternative to the individual writing, ESL children at the beginning stages of language acquisition may be placed in a small group of children, ideally with one child who is bilingual in the child's language and with other children who speak fluent English, but are compassionate and helpful.

Guidelines for Using Literacy Scaffolds

By using literacy scaffolds such as the ones contained in this book, all children can write poetry if the teacher carefully uses the procedures described in the *Cats* poem lesson:

- Read an example (or several examples) of the poem that has a structure that can be easily emulated. Present the poem on the chalkboard or overhead projector while reading it; follow with a choral reading.

- Ask children to articulate what they notice about the specific structural features of the poem. Add information about specific poetic conventions as appropriate for the age, ability, and linguistic competence of the group.
- Choose a topic for a similar poem that will fit into the structure of the original poem.
- Have children brainstorm some words or phrases that might be used in the poem.
- Solicit individual lines for the poem, writing them clearly on the chalkboard or overhead projector.
- Read the finished product chorally with children.
- Invite children to now write their own poem, individually or in small cooperative groups, using the literacy scaffold as needed. (Be sure to point out to the children that they are free to deviate from the scaffold; it is only a guide.)

Additionally, to successfully launch a poetry writing program, follow these few essential suggestions (Koch 1980):
- All poetry should be assigned and written in school. This way, it is never considered drudgery, but rather a refreshing departure from the classroom routine. Moreover, when creating in class, children have an opportunity to share their excitement with classmates in what can easily become a "community of poets." Of course, if some children then *choose* to write poetry outside of school, the implication is that those children have transferred the enthusiasm for writing poetry to other places and times in their lives. This is no less than a cause for celebration!
- Do not ask or expect children to consistently rhyme their poems. While repetition is quite natural for children, rhyming can become an onerous chore that can

interfere with what a child is really trying to say. For the limited English-proficient child, moreover, rhyming may be the straw that breaks the camel's back; it requires too much agility with the language. It is suggested, therefore, that many models of both rhymed as well as unrhymed poems, such as those contained in this text, be offered to children as scaffolds so that they receive the message that an unrhymed poem is absolutely acceptable.

- As children are writing poetry, allow them to walk around the classroom reading and discussing other children's poetry. Besides the obvious "languaging" that occurs as a bonus to limited English speakers, children also become inspired by the ideas and word choices of their classmates and may wish to borrow some. To assure that such practice is perceived as "borrowing" and not "stealing," inform the class that such behavior is quite flattering to the idea's originator and thus perfectly legitimate as long as the originator is acknowledged.

- Make certain that the classroom environment is absolutely safe for risk-taking, which is the optimal atmosphere in which a child can acquire either a first or a second language. This safety factor implies that no one—not even the teacher—may correct or negatively criticize a child's poem. Children must be taught to listen carefully and empathetically to each other's poems. They may then ask for clarification if there is a line that they do not understand, or they may request elaboration if they wish to hear even *more* about the subject. The audience for a poem, whether it is the teacher or a small group of children, needs only to know to attempt to understand and appreciate what the poet is saying.

- Free children to write in their own special words—and not what they believe the adult world, or the academic world, wishes to hear—by carefully explaining to them that poems can be "crazy" (as opposed to "silly," which may be perceived as a pejorative term), or "real." Such a preface will prevent children from offering such hackneyed lines as "the sky is blue and my heart is too," as they attempt to conform to what they believe to be the sophisticated and serious nature of poetry. Moreover, this freedom to speak in their own words should refer as well to "code switching," as children are encouraged to use words from both English and their primary language to express themselves in the richest and most spontaneous way possible.

• Consider some guidelines for "appropriate" topics for sharing. Because of the expressive, indeed, often cathartic nature of poetry writing, revealing or even disturbing poems are often shared with the class. Intimate details about children's home lives often surface that may provide important insights for teachers as to the needs of individual writers. For example, a poem written by one eleven-year-old girl (page 85) concerns her obvious fears about her weight, which may or may not signify an incipient eating disorder. Such a poem could be discussed privately with the child to determine if professional help should be sought. On the other hand, some children may use poetry as a forum to shock others, so the teacher may wish to create some general guidelines concerning inappropriate language, graphic violence, sex, or personal attacks on others.

Compiling Original Poetry Anthologies

When children have spent several months writing many different types of poems, they are usually eager to compile some of their favorite poems into a book or selected anthology. Duthie and Zimet (1992) suggest that this gathering activity is, in itself, a highly creative activity with children being driven to make some very personal decisions about themes they wish to use and which poems they want to select.

To prepare children for compiling poetry for their individual anthologies, it may first be helpful to introduce them to a variety of existing anthologies, many of which are listed in appendix B. The teacher might point out the bases upon which he or she believes the poems were selected for several different anthologies, helping children to see the thread that weaves all the poems together; for example, in Leland Jacobs's *Poetry for Summer,* all poems relate to feelings about or events relating to that particular season.

Subsequently, children can be asked to look through their own portfolios of poems they have written to select several poems they feel have merit, and then decide upon a unifying theme for the poems to use as a title for the anthology. Conversely, they may choose to first select a theme based upon their favorite poem and then compose several more poems that relate to that theme.

When the poems have been edited and written neatly on quality paper, the children may wish to add illustrations. Lamination of the pages culminates in the creation of a poetry anthology, offering a product that is both attractive and durable. The children's anthologies can then be circulated around the room for browsing and free reading and shared with classmates, guests, and parents.

How to Use This Book

In the following pages the preservice and practicing teacher will find numerous poem ideas, or literacy scaffolds. In other words, each poem presented has a clear, explicable structure that can be shown to children and then imitated by them, so that they can easily write their own poetry using their own ideas and perceptions of the world. Each poem idea includes a description that explains the structure that is to be imitated, and a lead-in activity to help the teacher get the students motivated and mentally set for the poetry writing session. Included with the poem idea are two examples—original poems that have been created by real children in diverse classrooms using the literacy scaffold. Some activities are based on published poems by well-known poets. These originals can be found in appendix A, page 149. It is suggested that the teacher print each example poem on the chalkboard or overhead, read it chorally with the children, and then help children to identify the structure that is to be imitated. In some cases, no explanation is necessary.

The book is divided into two sections: primary and intermediate (these refer to the inherent difficulty of the poem idea, rather than the grade level). For children who have had limited experiences with poetry and for children in the early stages of English-language acquisition, begin with the primary poem ideas and progress hierarchically to the more advanced ones.

This book is for those teachers who see the heterogeneous gardens of children populating their classrooms not as obstacles to be overcome, but as positive and exciting challenges. Such teachers tend to be optimists and can see the possibilities for poetry where others might not. They realize that while all their students may not speak fluent English, poetry is the universal language of childhood. Children and poets are discoverers—of new ideas and of new ways to express them. The literacy scaffolds in this book provide the tools to help make these discoveries.

References

California Department of Education. "It's elementary!" In *Elementary Grades Task Force Report.* Sacramento, CA: California Department of Education, 1992.

Cecil, N. L. *Teaching to the Heart: An Affective Approach to Literacy Instruction.* Salem, WI: Sheffield Publishing Co., 1993.

Cecil, N. L., and P. Lauritzen. *Literacy and the Arts.* White Plains, NY: Longman Publishing Co., forthcoming 1994.

Denman, G. A. *When You've Made It Your Own: Teaching Poetry to Young People.* Portsmouth, NH: Heinemann, 1988.

Duthie, C., and K. Zimet. "Poetry is like directions for your imagination!" *The Reading Teacher* 46 (1992): 14–24.

Hoskisson, K., and G. E. Tompkins. *The Language Arts Curriculum: Content and Teaching Strategies.* Columbus, OH: Merrill Publishing Co., 1987.

Koch, K. *Wishes, Lies, and Dreams: Teaching Children to Write Poetry.* New York: Harper & Row, 1980.

Middleton-Moz, J. *Children of Trauma: Rediscovering Your Discarded Self.* Deerfield Beach, FL: Health Communications, 1989.

Shapiro, S. "Beyond the anthology: Poetry readings in the classroom." In N. Cecil (Ed.), *Literacy in the '90s: Selected Readings in the Language Arts.* Dubuque, IA: Kendall/Hunt, 1990.

Stewig, J. W. "Choral speaking: Who has the time? Why take the time?" *Childhood Education* 57 (1981): 25–29.

Tiedt, S. W., and I. M. Tiedt. *Elementary Teachers' New Complete Idea Handbook.* Boston: Allyn & Bacon, 1987.

Part I

Primary Scaffolds

I Wish…

(Koch 1980)

Description

Every line begins with the words "I wish." There are no set number of lines. Game-like "rules"—such as each line must contain a color, a cartoon character, a country, an emotion, a season, a famous person—may be added.

Lead-in Activity

Have the children name some things that they have wished upon, and list their answers on the chalkboard. For example, ask: "Who has wished on a star/a four-leaf clover/a rabbit's foot/birthday candles?" and so on. Chorally chant the poem that children often say when they see a star at night:

> Star light, star bright,
> First star I see tonight.
> I wish I may, I wish I might,
> Have the wish I wish tonight.

Ask children to share some of the things they have wished for. Tell them they will be writing a poem that tells about lots of fanciful things that they can wish for. Write a group poem with "rules"; for example, a color and an emotion have to be in each line. Read the following poems aloud to the students. Finally, have each child write an "I Wish" poem using the following scaffold:

First line: I wish _____;
Repeat as often as desired.
Last line: And I wish _____.

I Wish #1
(using a color, place, and cartoon characters)

I wish I were on the Red Sea with Mother Goose and Grimm;
I wish I could go to Paris in my blue dress and meet
    Donald Duck;
I wish my parents would take me to Disneyland so I could talk
    to Snow White;
I wish I had some pink shoes to show the Pink Panther in
    Puerto Rico;
And I wish I weren't so blue just like Charlie Brown when he
    goes to the Pumpkin Patch on Halloween.

— Bonnie, grade 3

I Wish #2
(using an emotion and a famous person)

I wish I wasn't so angry with Santa Claus about forgetting
    my Barbie;
I wish I could not be so jealous of Madonna;
I wish Janet Jackson would like me and be my friend;
I wish I could stop being afraid of Freddy Krueger—
    He gives me nightmares;
I wish M.C. Hammer would come to Cleveland and make
    me happy;
I wish Axl Rose would come to a party and make me laugh;
And I wish Princess Diana would fall in love with
    her prince again.

— Daphne, grade 3

2 I Like…

Description

This poem consists of couplets that concern children's likes and dislikes. There are no set number of couplets. The first line begins with "I like." The following line begins with "But I *don't* like" and may be related to the topic of the first line.

Lead-in Activity

Have the students listen to "These Are A Few Of My Favorite Things" from *The Sound of Music.* List the singer's favorite things on the chalkboard as they are recalled. Invite children to add their *own* favorite things to the list, expanding it to include certain actions, situations, or behaviors of people that are pleasing to them. For each of the brainstormed items, ask the children if they can think of a downside to the item or action; for example, "I like gentle raindrops, but I don't like thunderstorms with loud crashing thunder that wakes me up in the middle of the night." Provide each child with a photocopied sheet containing the following scaffold:

I like _____,
But I don't like _____.
Repeat as often as desired.

As a class, write a group poem soliciting a response from each child. Then read aloud the following examples and have the children write their own "I Like" poems.

I Like #1

I like it when you talk quietly with me,
But I don't like it when you shout at me.
I like it when it rains and everything smells fresh,
But I don't like it when it pours for days and I can't go out
    and play.
I like it when my dog is glad to see me and he runs up to
    say hello,
But I don't like it when he jumps on me and gets my
    clothes dirty.
I like it when I'm looking forward to something—
    like Christmas,
But I don't like it when it's all over and then I have to wait
    364 days until *next* Christmas!

— Jamal, grade 3

I Like #2

I like buzz cuts,
But I don't like them so short that they look stupid.
I like hamburgers,
But I don't like the really fat kind you can't get your
    mouth around.
I like recess,
But I don't like it when it's freezing cold outside.
I like to go fishing with my dad,
But I don't like it when he brings his buddy and forgets
    about me.
I like weekends,
But I don't like them when Mom says,
"We have lots and lots of work to be done this weekend!"

— Devon, grade 3

3 I'm So Smart

Description

This type of poem is an excellent self-esteem builder. There are no set number of lines. Each line begins with "I'm so smart." The poem can be written tongue-in-cheek or as a real record of what children have accomplished or are capable of doing.

Lead-in Activity

Using scrap paper, have the children make a list of all the things they can do (for example, cook, sew, paint, speak another language, do dishes, rake leaves, write, sing, dance, and so on). On pieces of tagboard, have children draw outlines of themselves, cut them out, and decorate them to look like themselves. Ask them to transfer their lists of accomplishments to the backs of their cutout figures. Hang these by string from the ceiling over each student's desk. Reinforce the idea that "we have a roomful of marvelous human resources and potential" to inspire self-worth. Read the following "I'm So Smart" poems aloud, then encourage the children to use ideas from their hanging figures to help them write their own poems. The following scaffold will guide them:

First line: I'm so smart _____ .
Repeat as often as desired.
Last line: And I'm so smart _____ .

I'm So Smart #1

I'm so smart I can beat my baby sister at checkers.
I'm so smart I can read a book upside down.
I'm so smart I can comb my hair with my fingers.
I'm so smart I can beat my turtle in a running race.
I'm so smart I can tell what we're having for dinner
    without even looking.
And I'm so smart I wrote this poem!

— *Pedro, grade 2*

I'm So Smart #2

I'm so smart I could set the table when I was six.
I'm so smart I can help my dad wash the car.
I'm so smart I can speak Spanish *and* English.
I'm so smart I earned $2.85 selling lemonade.
I'm so smart I can swim across the YMCA pool four times
    in a row.
And I'm so smart I can teach you to do these things too!

— *Angela, grade 3*

4 When You Tell Me

Description

This poetic format offers a cathartic way to deal with verbal rebukes through writing. It is similar to the "I Like" poem (page 20) in that it deals with expressing feelings; however, this poem deals more specifically with responses to the spoken words of others. The first line is a verbal stimulus, "When you tell me"; while the second line is the poet's emotional response to the verbal stimulus. The third line is a contrasting stimulus, "But when you tell me"; while the fourth line offers the emotional response to that stimulus.

Lead-in Activity

Discuss the term *antonym* with the children. Write *happy, sad, angry, calm, unafraid,* and *afraid* on the chalkboard or overhead. Sitting in a circle, have children take turns selecting one of the words to use in a sentence stem that they can complete any way they wish; for example, "I feel angry when…" After each child has contributed a sentence, group the children in pairs. Have one child in the pair make up a sentence that includes one of the words for which there is an antonym and have the other child in the pair respond in the opposite manner using the antonym of the first child's word. For example, the first child might say, "I feel angry when our recess is canceled because of rain," leading the second child to respond, "But I feel happy when I find out we get to have a popcorn party in the cafeteria instead of going outside." Encourage each pair of students to share their sentences with the rest of the class. Read the following aloud to the class. Then have each student write a "When You Tell Me" poem using the following scaffold:

Line 1: When you (tell/ask) me _____,
Line 2: I feel _____ and _____;
Line 3: But when you [*opposite to first line*],
Line 4: I feel _____ and _____.

When You Tell Me #1

When you tell me you like me,
I feel happy and I smile;
But when you tell me you *don't* like me,
I feel sad and I want to cry.

— Josh, grade 2

When You Tell Me #2

When you ask me to join in a game of kickball,
I feel included and excited;
But when you tell me I can't play with you,
I feel angry and I really hope you lose!

— Carmen, grade 4

5 If It Weren't For You

(Adapted from If It Weren't For You *by Charlotte Zolotow)*

Description

This poem addresses issues of love/hate, ambiguity, and resentment that are present in any relationship, but also the joy. Each line concerns what the child could do if a parent, teacher, sibling, and so on, was not directly involved in his or her life. The last line of the poem is a reversal of feelings and underscores what the child would miss *without* that person in his or her life.

Lead-in Activity

Discuss the term *relationship* with the children. Ask them if they think it is possible to feel positive about a friend or relative *all* the time. Do friends or relatives ever say or do things that are annoying or upsetting? Place two columns on the chalkboard or overhead. At the top of one column write "Positive Words or Actions" and above the other column write "Negative Words or Actions." Have students assess their relationship with a friend or relative, describing words or actions that are loving and/or enriching in one column, while identifying those words and actions that are annoying and/or restrictive in the other column. Read the book *If It Weren't For You* to the students.[1] Then read the following poems to show how such ambiguous feelings provide excellent fodder for poetry. Finally, have the children write their own poems using the following scaffold to guide them:

---

1. Charlotte Zolotow. *If It Weren't for You.* New York: Harper & Row, 1966.

Line 1: If it weren't for you, [*person*],

Line 2: _____ ;

Repeat as often as desired.

Second last line: But if it weren't for you, [*same person*],

Last line: _____ .

If It Weren't For You #1

If it weren't for you, teacher,
I could play Nintendo all day long;
If it weren't for you, teacher,
I wouldn't have homework and could watch more TV;
If it weren't for you, teacher,
I wouldn't have to read that boring social studies book;
But if it weren't for you, teacher,
I'd know lots less than I do now!

— *Alejándro, grade 3*

If It Weren't For You #2

If it weren't for you, Little Brother,
I would never have to close my bedroom door.
If it weren't for you, Little Brother,
I could watch Clarissa without being disturbed.
If it weren't for you, Little Brother,
I could go trick or treating with my girlfriends.
If it weren't for you, Little Brother,
All my toys would be in one piece—especially my dolls.
But if it weren't for you, Little Brother,
Christmas wouldn't be as much fun because
No one would believe in Santa Claus anymore.

— *Lydia, grade 3*

6 Colors

(Koch 1980)

Description

A color poem can be executed in two ways: each line can begin with a description of the same color, or each line could describe a different color. Each line may begin with the sentence stem, "Green is as green as" or a simpler format, "Green is like."

Lead-in Activity

Ask children to select a color. Write the color word in a circle in the center of the chalkboard or overhead. Encourage children to brainstorm some words, feelings, phrases, and ideas that they associate with the chosen color. Cluster these words in circles connected to the original circle by lines. After reading the example poems, have the children write a color poem as a group, with as many children as want to contributing lines. Then have the students write their own poems. Following are two scaffolds they can use to guide them:

First line: [*Color*] is like _____ ;
Repeat as often as desired.
Last line: And [*same color*] is _____ .

or

First line: [*Color*] is as [*same color*] as_____ ;
Repeat as often as desired.
Last line: And [*color*] is as [*same color*] as_____ .

Green (Color Poem #1)

Green is like a great big dill pickle;
Green is like a field of grass dotted with daisies;
Green is like a wave of feeling when someone gets something
   you wanted;
Green is like the woods on a camping trip in June;
And green is like leaves without the flowers.

                 — Ali, grade 3

Colors (Color Poem #2)

Pink is as pink as a wild cloud of bubble gum;
Green is as green as a stomachache;
Orange is as orange as your sunglasses make it;
Blue is as blue as a night in Antarctica;
Brown is as brown as the hot desert wind;
And red is as red as a surprise birthday party.

                 — Simone, grade 3

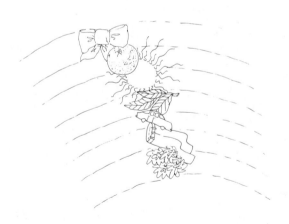

7 If I Were...

Description

This poem starts out with the phrase "If I were," followed by anything a child can imagine: animal, hero, cartoon or book character, villain, and so on. The next line provides the answer to what the poet would do if he or she were that animal, hero, and so on.

Lead-in Activity

Ask the children to take a moment to think about an animal that they would like to be. Have them close their eyes and think about the first thing they would do if they were to become that animal. On the chalkboard or over-head, write:

If I were a _____,
I would _____.

Ask one of the children to fill in the blanks telling what animal he or she would be, and what he or she would do if he or she were that animal. Solicit responses from other children to add other couplets to the poem. Read the following poems aloud to inspire the children. Then have the children write their own poems using as many couplets as they wish.

[handwritten margin notes:]
To one as a class first write on overhead students choose a picture.
- do a rough copy first
- cartridge paper for good copy

If I Were a Spider (If I Were Poem #1)

If I were a spider,
I would spin an enormous web and catch Volkswagens.
If I were a spider,
I would buy four pairs of shoes and learn to tap dance.
If I were a spider,
I would call myself "Mommy Short Legs."

— Tanya, grade 3

What I Would Do (If I Were Poem #2)

If I were a painting on a wall,
I would stare back at the people staring at me.
If I were a tomato,
I would lie in the sun all day growing red and juicy.
If I were a teddy bear,
I would have a soul and love a little boy like he loved me.
If I were a flower,
I would want to be the prettiest so I'd be picked first.
If I were a tiger,
I'd kill all the bad people in the world and leave everyone else
　　in peace.

— Jasmine, grade 3

8 Give Me...

Description

This poem helps children realize that the things they want may be both material and nonmaterial in nature. For younger or less experienced poets, this poem can be written simply, with each line beginning with the sentence stem, "Give me" and going on to express what the poet wishes to be given. For older or more experienced poets, the poem may consist of lines that alternate between tangible and intangible items.

Lead-in Activity

Write on the chalkboard or overhead the words *tangible* and *intangible.* Explain to children that tangible things can be seen and/or touched, while intangible items are invisible to the eye and cannot be touched. Solicit a list of items that can go under each heading. Seat children in a circle. Ask each child to begin with the phrase, "Give me," alternating between a tangible and an intangible item. Read the following poems aloud to show children how their sentences can become a group poem. Have the children write their own poems.

Give Me #1
(any items)

Give me a pony and a week off from school to ride him;
Give me a hundred chocolate mint cookies that I don't have
    to share with my brother and sisters;
Give me a shiny new bike with ten speeds, at least;
Give me all the Hawaiian pizza I can eat;
Give me a pair of black roller blades with fluorescent laces,
And give me a check for a million dollars so I can buy these
    things with change for my dad.

                                          — Gus, grade 3

Give Me #2
(tangible and intangible alternating)

Give me a sunny day in April after a soft spring rain;
Give me a great big bunch of fragrant lilacs;
Give me peace everywhere in the world;
Give me a white dove of peace;
Give me a chance to help someone;
Give me a strong body and a strong mind;
Give me a trip all around the world,
Give me a ticket and I'll go.

                                        — Carmen, grade 3

9 What Am I Like?

Description

This poem involves self-reflection. Give the children a series of questions that involve making a choice between two ideas, to decide which one they are more like. The first line of the poem is the question—the scaffold provided by the question. The children's answers—their individual responses—become the alternating line.

Lead-in Activity

Put several choice questions on sentence strips, one strip for each child in the class. (The following questions work well: Are you more like the sun or the moon? Day or night? An earthquake or a volcano? Snow or rain? The ocean or the mountains? A dog or a cat? Cotton or wool? Summer or winter?) Ask the children to select a question and give them a few minutes to think about their responses. In small share groups, encourage them to tell their classmates their choice and the reasons they chose as they did. Read the following poems aloud to illustrate how the questions and answers can create interesting poetry. Then have the children write their own poems. They can use the following scaffold to guide them:

Line 1: Am I like _____ or _____?
Line 2: I am like _____ (for/because)_____ .
Repeat as often as desired.

What Am I Like? #1

Am I like the gentle rain or a flood?
I am like a flood for I do things quickly and in a hurry.
Am I like the summer or the winter?
I am like the summer for I am long and lazy and love the sun.
Am I like day or like night?
I am like the day for I thrive on noise and movement and life.
Am I like the city or the country?
I am like the city for I'm always looking for new places
    to go and new people to meet.

— Cynthia, grade 3

What Am I Like? #2

Am I more like cotton or wool?
I am like cotton because I'm cool and always ready to go.
Am I more like a dog or a cat?
I am like a cat because cats are happy to be by themselves.
Am I more like a sunrise or a sunset?
I am more like a sunrise because I'm always ready to greet
    the day.
Am I more like a car or a truck?
I am more like a truck because I can go in the mountains,
I am strong, and I'm helpful to people.
Am I more like gold or silver?
I am more like gold because I am worth a lot to my parents,
    family, and friends.

— Tyler, grade 3

Transitions

(Koch 1980)

Description

This type of poem is a natural self-esteem builder. The poem is written in triplets: the first line begins with "I used to be"; the second line begins with "I became"; and the concluding line begins with "Now." This pattern helps children to reflect on how much they have "grown up" over the years.

Lead-in Activity

Write the word *change* on the chalkboard or overhead. Ask children to think of some specific ways they have changed since they were babies. Invite children to respond to this question, beginning with the sentence stem, "I used to be." As children share their reflections, ask them to compare their answers with their feelings about how they are now. What do they think caused the changes in their behavior or status? What were some of the events that caused the changes? After everyone who wishes to has shared their reflections, read the following transition poems aloud. Have the students write their own poems based on the following scaffold:

Line 1: I used to be _____;
Line 2: I became _____;
Line 3: Now _____.
Repeat.

Change (Transition Poem #1)

I used to be shy;
I became talkative;
Now I'm a chatterbox and everyone's friend.

I used to be afraid of the dark;
I became less afraid as I camped in the woods;
Now I love the peace and quiet of the night.

— *Kanti, grade 3*

Transitions (Transition Poem #2)

I used to be a picky eater, my mom says.
I became a kid who would try any food.
Now I eat everything in sight!

I used to like "Sesame Street" best of all TV shows;
I became a fan of "Full House";
Now my favorite show is "Beverly Hills 90210."

— *Jennifer, grade 3*

I Remember

(Koch 1980)

Description

Children begin each line of the poem with a memory, using the sentence stem "I remember." Lines may alternate between good memories and bad ones, or may consist entirely of one or the other. The poem consisting of unhappy memories may be cathartic in effect, while the good memory poem may provide an upbeat recollection of a happier time. As an alternative, the poem can be written as a character in a book might reflect upon his or her life.

Lead-in Activity

Read the following poems aloud. Ask children to close their eyes and "walk" them around the first place they remember living in (it's fine if they have lived in the same residence their whole life). Invite them to go through each room, taking note of the furniture, the light from the windows, the pictures hanging up, the aroma from the kitchen, and so on. Take them through their bedroom and have them revisit their closet, bed, dresser, lamp, and so on. Then take them outside to their backyard and ask them what season it is and what trees, bushes, flowers, they see. Bring them back into their living room and ask them to think of a special time or event that occurred there. When they open their eyes, have them write an "I Remember" poem, using their memories.

I Remember #1

I remember the fireplace in our family room with its warm
    friendly glow.
I remember chats with my aunts in the kitchen while they all
    helped to prepare dinner.
I remember my sister and I staying up talking and laughing
    all night on Christmas Eve.
I remember sitting on the front porch counting the cars until
    Daddy came home.
I remember playing "Capture the Flag" in the backyard until
    it got dark and we had to go in.
I remember looking out my bedroom window to the street
    below feeling warm and snug in my bed.

— David, grade 4

Poems can also be written in response to literature. In this
poem, Esther is writing as Tough Boy, the main character
in *Tough Boy & Sister,* might have written it:

I Remember #2

I remember fishing on the river with my father;
I remember my mother dying and Sister and I being very sad
    and frightened.
I remember my father telling us we could still live with him,
Even though the nosy neighbors didn't think it was wise.
I remember feeling very, very close to Sister as we huddled in
    the cold, damp dark.
I remember my father leaving for town and wondering if he
    would ever return.
I remember feeling proud of Sister and proud of myself when
    we realized we had both learned how to survive.

— Esther, grade 4

12 Definitions

Description

This free-verse poem can consist of any number of lines. Students select a state of being (for example, happiness, loneliness, sadness), or an animal, relationship, season, sibling, and so on, of their choice. They then define that entity by free associating their personal feelings and reactions to it. As an alternative, every other line can state what the entity is not.

Lead-in Activity

Select a common state of being about which to brainstorm with children. Some possible topics are happiness, anger, jealousy, loneliness, or confusion. Younger children may feel more comfortable using concrete entities such as tigers, beaches, friends, brothers, shoes, and so on. To provide additional ways to think about the word, ask children: "What is it? What is it like? What is it *not* like? What are some examples of it?" With the students' input, write a group poem on the chalkboard. Read the following poems aloud and then have the children select their own word to write a poem about.

Loneliness (Definition Poem #1)

Loneliness is long boring days without anyone to play with.
Loneliness is *not* having a good friend over to spend the night.
Loneliness is a Saturday afternoon by yourself
When everyone else is at Tiffany's birthday party.
Loneliness is watching everyone playing ball in the street
When you're doing your homework.
Loneliness is listening to everyone talk in another language
And not understanding a single word.
Loneliness is just an awful feeling of being too alone.

— *Franco, grade 3*

Puppies (Definition Poem #2)

Puppies are big wet kisses all over your face.
Puppies are messes on the carpet that someone has to clean up.
Puppies are little animals that love you no matter what you
    look like or what you have done.
Puppies are beasts that whine and cry all night 'til you go and
    pet them.
Puppies are soft and furry with big eyes and huge clumsy feet
    that are too big for them.
Puppies mean that someone has to feed them, take them for
    walks, and make sure they're not sick.
Puppies are cute and loving and definitely worth the bother!

— *Brittany, grade 3*

13 Someday

Description

Each couplet begins with "Someday" and expresses something that the child hopes might happen in the future. Couplets may alternate between what a child will *have* and what a child will *do*. "Do" lines begin with "I will."

Lead-in Activity

Write the word *future* on the chalkboard or overhead. Cluster ideas that children offer about what the word means to them. Make two columns on the chalkboard: "have" and "do." Ask children to brainstorm some material items they think they might possess someday. Place these in the first column. Next, ask children to consider some activities, hobbies, or careers they might pursue (or do) in the future and place these in the second column. Then have the children make a group poem. Read the following poems aloud. Finally, have the children write their own poems.

Someday #1

Someday I will own a sleek forty-foot sailboat.
I will fish from the boat and take all my friends
Sailing, and fishing, and sunning themselves.
Someday I will have a huge pink house high on a hill
With a Christmas-tree forest in the backyard.
I will allow all the homeless people in the city to camp
In the woods in my backyard.
Someday I will have a white-maned Appaloosa.
I will take her for gallops on the beach
And we will ride together watching the sunset.
Someday I will have a pair of shiny green roller blades.
I will leave the other kids behind while I skate like the wind.

— Van, grade 3

Someday #2

Someday I will have a paper route.
I will wake up early in the morning and deliver the paper
To all the people in the neighborhood.
Someday I will have lots of friends and boyfriends.
I will be a cheerleader and go to parties with my boyfriend.
Someday I will have a red Ferrari and everyone will want
    a ride in it.
I will ask all my friends to pick a number
And the ones with the highest number can ride with me.
Someday I will have my own TV.
I will never have to fight with my brother over whether to watch
    "Clarissa" or stupid football.

— Ellen, grade 3

# Word Pictures

Description

In this free-verse poem the children carefully observe an object (a paper clip, shoe, cup, telephone, pencil, and so on) and then describe it and tell about its function, without using words that reveal the object's identity. The last line usually contains a sound associated with the object.

Lead-in Activity

Hide a well-known object, such as a pair of scissors, in a paper bag. Without mentioning what the object is, describe the object that is in the bag, then ask the children to try to guess what it is. Have the children select a commonly used object. Ask them how they might describe it to someone who has never seen such an object (either because the person is blind or is from a culture where the object is not used). Solicit words and phrases children might use to help the person "see" the object and write these on the chalkboard. Using the words, write a group poem on the board. Next, read the following poems aloud, then have the children write their own poems about objects of their choice.

Scissors (Word-Picture Poem #1)

Long, sharp, and made of metal or plastic;
They cut paper and cardboard.
Two round circles just right so I can
Put my fingers in them.
They open and close, open and close.
Snip, snap! Snip, snap!

— Emily, grade 3

Fan (Word-Picture Poem #2)

Four blades look like mice's ears.
Round and round they go.
Cools us off in the summer by giving us a pretend
   cool breeze.
Messes up my hair and blows papers around.
A soft whirr, whirr, whirr.

— Dustin, grade 3

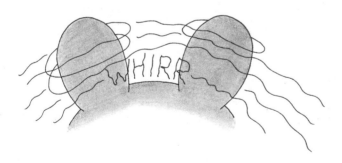

15 Comparisons

Description

Using simple similes, children can write interesting poems comparing common items with whatever enters their minds. Every line contains this implicit comparison. An entire poem may contain many similes about one subject, or each line may contain a new subject with its own simile.

Lead-in Activity

Explain the term *simile* to the children and give some examples from common speech (such as "skinny as a rail") or from children's literature. Group children in pairs and ask them to think of appropriate similes to describe the following items to someone who has never seen or experienced them: spaghetti, grass, Jell-O, orange, lightning, rain, love, bee sting. Write a group poem using the students' responses. Read the following poems aloud, then have the children write their own comparison poems.

Comparison Poem #1

Spaghetti is like slimy brains;
An orange is like a tangy surprise;
A telephone is like a voice telescope;
Rain is like a watering can in the sky;
Love is like some warm sunshine that feels happy.

— Daniel, grade 3

Comparison Poem #2

Grass is like a long velvety carpet of green;
Grass is like a strong smell of spring when someone
    just mowed it.
Grass is like hay only springy and not scratchy.
Grass is like a blanket for the ground.
And grass is like a big green bed to lie on
And look up at the stars.

— Henryk, grade 3

16 Double Takes

Description

This series of couplets is a simple reflection on misconceptions; they show students how first impressions can often be misleading. The first line of the poem begins, "I thought I heard (saw, smelled, felt, tasted)" and so on; the second line reveals the error to the reader: "I turned around and found it was only…"

Lead-in Activity

Discuss how sometimes people see/hear/feel something and too quickly jump to conclusions about its meaning. For example, someone may think they heard someone moaning, but find it was only the wind; similarly, someone may think they see a seal in the ocean, but find it is only a log. Invite children to share some experiences they have had of this nature. Explain that these "double takes" make interesting poetry and demonstrate this by reading the following poems:

Double Take #1

I thought I saw a UFO in the sky.
I turned around and found it was only my friend's Frisbee.
I thought I heard my mother calling me.
I turned around and found it was only my neighbor
    calling her dog!
I thought I saw a sign that said, "Orange."
I turned around and found that it said, "Open."
I thought I heard a seagull's cry.
I turned around and found that it was only a baby crying
    from the house next door.

— Nuri, grade 3

Double Take #2

I thought I saw an angel in the sky,
Shining, fluttering, as bright as the sun.
I turned around and found it was only a huge piece of
    aluminum foil.
I thought I heard somebody being shot.
I turned around and realized it was just a firecracker.
It's the Fourth of July!
I thought I smelled a forest fire burning.
I turned around and realized it was only the next-door
    neighbor burning leaves.
I thought I saw my teacher shopping at the mall.
I turned around and it was only a grumpy lady who looks just
    like her—everyone has a twin!

— Jennifer, grade 3

I Like Bugs

(Adapted from Bugs *by Margaret Wise Brown)*

Description

This prescribed format is easy for young children, or children for whom English is a second language, to copy. Read Margaret Wise Brown's poem, *Bugs,* to the children (see page 149, appendix A). After they are familiar with the poem, have them select a plural noun and describe it in the same way that the bugs are described in the original poem.

Lead-in Activity

Ask children if they like bugs. Have them give reasons why or why not. Show them a picture of a beetle or some other bug. Let them use all the words they can think of to describe this bug. Ask them where they might find such a bug. Provide children with a literacy scaffold, such as the following, that allows them to fill in their own ideas:

I like _____ .
Any kind of _____ .
Bad _____ , mean _____ , round _____ ,
Green _____ , fat _____ .
A_____ in a _____ .
A_____ on the _____ .
A_____ in the_____ .
A_____ in the_____ .
Buggy_____ , black _____ .
Any kind of_____ .
I like _____ .

Later, encourage children to change the adjectives (describing words) to those that more closely describe their chosen subject. Allow children to illustrate their poems and incorporate them into a class book.

I Like Grasshoppers (I Like Poem #1)

I like grasshoppers.
Any kind of grasshopper.
Bad grasshoppers, mean grasshoppers, round grasshoppers.
Green grasshoppers, fat grasshoppers.
A grasshopper in a field,
A grasshopper on the fence,
A grasshopper in the kitchen,
A grasshopper in the car.
Buggy grasshoppers, shiny grasshoppers,
Big grasshoppers, black grasshoppers.
Any kind of grasshopper.
I like grasshoppers.

— *Craig, grade 1*

I Like Pizza (I Like Poem #2)

I like pizza.
Any kind of pizza.
Pepperoni pizza, sausage pizza, Hawaiian pizza,
Large pizza, personal pan pizza.
A pizza in a restaurant,
A pizza in a kitchen.
A pizza for lunch,
A pizza for dinner.
Cheesy pizza, garlicky, mushroomy pizza.
Hot pizza, cold pizza,
Any kind of pizza.
I like pizza.

— *Ralph, grade 1*

18 Apologies

Description

The first line of this poem begins with a tongue-in-cheek "I'm sorry" and addresses, in a whimsical way, some inanimate object that may have been inadvertently violated or offended through use or abuse. For example, apologies can be offered to chairs because we have sat in them, to flowers because we have picked them, to refrigerators because we have raided them, or to doormats because we have wiped our feet on them. The last line of the poem asks for forgiveness.

Lead-in Activity

Encourage pairs of children to volunteer to do a re-enactment of an apology scene where one apologizes to the other for something that was done accidentally. Ask children if they have ever considered apologizing to inanimate objects that they use every day. Read the poems below aloud and as a group write an apology poem. Then help children brainstorm other items about which they can write their own poems of apology.

I'm Sorry #1

I'm sorry, Daisy.
I just saw you swaying in the wind
Looking all yellow and white and pretty.
And I just had to pull your head off.
I'm really sorry, Daisy. Did it hurt a lot?
I needed to find out if Jared likes me.
So I pulled off all your petals, one by one.
I'm sorry, Daisy.
Will you ever forgive me?

— Adrienne, grade 3

I'm Sorry #2

I'm sorry, Doormat.
I got your nice bristles all dirty
When I wiped my feet on you after I
Walked through that awesome mud puddle.
I'm sorry, Doormat,
I put my huge size three feet all over you.
I'm sorry, Doormat.
I left you out in the cold all winter long
And let all the neighbors rub ice and snow
All over you.
I'm sorry, Doormat.
Will you ever forgive me?

— Ronald, grade 3

19 Two Worders

Description

Each line in this poem can contain only two words. A separate thought about the chosen topic is expressed in each line. Chosen topics may be autobiographical, about pets, schools, relatives, classmates, feelings, seasons, sports, favorite toys. Topics could be integrated with science or social studies units (for example, whales, the solar system, or Mexico).

Lead-in Activity

This poetry-writing session may be preceded by an art project. Brainstorm a variety of topics. Use one of the topics to do a group poem. Give the children pieces of construction paper and have them draw a picture of their topic on the bottom half of the paper. Then have the children describe the picture on the top half of the paper using two-word phrases, as demonstrated in the following poems.

Chrissy (Two-Worders Poem #1)

Loves Barbies
Rides bike
Many friends
All kinds
Wants kitten
Any color
Hates spinach
Eats anyway.

— *Chrissy, grade 3*

Whales (Two-Worders Poem #2)

Huge mammals,
Spout water,
Live young,
Drink milk.
Gentle creatures,
Ocean home.

— *Daniel, grade 3*

Holidays

Description

This somewhat more complex poem format contains seven lines and consists of features involving the five senses:

Line 1: [*Name of chosen holiday*]
Line 2: [*Something one sees during the holiday*]
Line 3: [*Something one hears during the holiday*]
Line 4: [*Something one smells during the holiday*]
Line 5: [*Something one tastes during the holiday*]
Line 6: [*Something one feels during the holiday*]
Line 7: *Repeat first line.*

Lead-in Activity

As a prewriting activity, ask the children to name their favorite holidays and list them on the chalkboard. Then have them brainstorm words, phrases, and ideas that they associate with each holiday. Show format to the children and discuss the five senses (sight, hearing, smell, taste, and touch). Brainstorm words and phrases associated with each of the senses. Read aloud the poems below, then write a group holiday poem. Finally, encourage each child to select his or her favorite holiday and write a poem using the format provided.

Holiday Poem #1

Fourth of July
Firecrackers coloring the sky.
People saying, "Ooooh…aaah!"
Hot dogs and hamburgers sizzling on a grill,
Ice cream melting in your mouth.
Feeling happy to be with my family and friends.
Fourth of July.

— Miriam, grade 3

Holiday Poem #2

Halloween
Witches, ghosts, and goblins out in the streets.
"Trick or Treat!" they tell their neighbors.
Smells of popcorn, licorice, and candy apples.
The best houses give chocolate candy bars.
Ooooooh…my aching tummy!
Halloween.

— Alana, grade 3

21 Lonely Letter

Description

This format, for more experienced poets, introduces alliteration and encourages vocabulary enhancement. A topic is chosen and descriptive words, all beginning with the same letter, are used to tell about the topic in the following way:

[Topic]
[*Topic/s*] are [*descriptive word beginning with the same letter*],
[*Topic/s*] are [*descriptive word beginning with the same letter*].
_____ , _____ , [*Eight words that describe the topic*
_____ , _____ . *and also begin with the same first letter*]
_____ , _____ ,
_____ , _____ .
[*Topic/s*] are _____ , [*Same words as beginning*
[*Topic/s*] are _____ . *couplet, but reversed*]

Lead-in Activity

Explain alliteration to the children in the following way: Ask them to pick a topic, such as turtles. Have them think of as many words as they can to describe turtles, making sure that all the words begin with the letter *t*. Try other topics, such a cookies, pets, snowmen, pickles, birds, and fish. Read the following poems aloud to the students, then, using the scaffold provided, write a group poem. Students can use dictionaries to help them find appropriate words. Finally, have the children write their own poems.

Teachers (Lonely Letter Poem #1)

Teachers are together,
Teachers are terrific.
Tough, talkative,
Tense, talented.
Teaching, toiling,
Terrifying, testy.
Teachers are terrific,
Teachers are together.

— *Jenna, grade 3*

Boys (Lonely Letter Poem #2)

Boys are bad,
Boys are beautiful.
Brave, bold,
Brainy, bright.
Bitter, bossy,
Backwards, bothersome.
Boys are beautiful,
Boys are bad.

— *Crystal, grade 3*

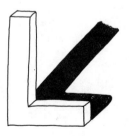

22 Triangular Triplets

Description

The triangular triplet poem uses three rhymed lines. The interesting characteristic of this poem is it can start with any of the lines and still make sense. The simple *a-a-a* format is not so demanding that it interferes with the ideas that the child is trying to express.

Lead-in Activity

Distribute colored construction paper and a sheet of plain white paper to each student. Ask them to draw pictures of themselves in the center of the white paper, participating in their favorite activity. Then instruct them to draw a triangle around their picture, cut it out, and paste it near the top of the construction paper. They can then use the picture in the triangle as inspiration for their three-lined rhymed poem. Each line of the poem can then be written on one side of the triangle, forming a "running commentary" about the activity inside the triangle:

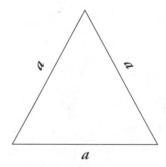

To demonstrate, read the following poems aloud:

Rollerblading (Triangular Triplet #1)

Yes, I love to Rollerblade,
In the sun or in the shade.
It's the fastest game I've ever played!

— *Laura, grade 2*

My Dog, Duke (Triangular Triplet #2)

I take my dog out for a run,
We stop and talk to everyone.
Duke and I have lots of fun!

— *Gregg, grade 1*

23 Numbers

Description

Integrating poetry and math, this format helps children understand simple math concepts. Each child selects a number from one to ten, then associates with that number in free-verse form. The poem is finished whenever the child runs out of ideas about the number.

Lead-in Activity

Introduce a number to children (for example, the number three) and provide several sets of objects that total that number. Ask the children to brainstorm all the ideas they can think of when they hear the number—a three-year-old sister and her behavior; often-heard saws such as "Three's a crowd" or "Three on a match"; the title of a movie such as *Three Men and a Baby;* a story such as "Goldilocks and the Three Bears." From all the brainstormed responses, develop a free-verse format for a group poem about the number. Read the following poems aloud to the children. Finally, have the children select the same or different number and, using the same procedure, write down their associations to create a number poem.

Four (Number Poem #1)

Four is an even number and can make a square.
Four is two pairs of friends playing a game;
Four is just before you can go to school,
Four is lots of babies—quadruplets!
And four is one more than three, but one less than five.

— Komae, grade 4

Six (Number Poem #2)

Six is losing your two front teeth and learning how to read,
Six is half a dozen and the biggest number on the dice,
Six is a nickel and one penny,
Six is enough kids to play kickball,
Six is two numbers in my telephone number,
And six is the first time when no one thinks you're a baby
    anymore!

— Bree, grade 3

24 Alliteration Numbers

(Tiedt & Tiedt 1987)

Description

This unrhymed poem is a fanciful exercise in alliteration. Each line contains a phrase about a number; line one concerns the number one and line ten is about the number ten. Each phrase contains a topic (noun), several descriptive words (adjectives beginning with the same sound, though not necessarily the same letter), as well as an action (verb) whimsically associated with the topic.

Lead-in Activity

Read children a line from one of the following poems and ask them what they notice about each word in the line (all the words begin with the same sound). To prepare them to write their own alliterative phrases, have them practice completing the following sentences out loud. Stress that the phrases or sentences need *not* make sense.

Six sad seals _____.
Four famous falcons _____.
Ten terrible turkeys _____.
Three thrilling thrushes _____.

Using the groups' brainstormed responses, write a group alliteration number poem. Finally, read the following poems and have the children write their own poems.

Numbers #1
(More complex; whole sentences; several adjectives)

One wacky warrior wants a wide weapon;
Two tiny toasters tug on a taxi;
Three thoughtful threads think about thunder;
Four fine fairies fear funny feet;
Five fabulous foxes find a favorite farm;
Six sandy servants save several cents;
Seven serious snakes seem so sassy;
Eight ugly oxen eat all the okra;
Nine nervous nachos need a number of nails;
Ten tacky toads tend a ton of tigers.

— *Rashona, grade 4*

Numbers #2
(Easier phrases with fewer descriptors)

One wise man watching a wand;
Two timid turtles tattling;
Three three-year-olds throwing thread;
Four forks fighting a family;
Five females fixing a fan;
Six seals seeing the sun;
Seven salmon singing a song;
Eight airplanes up in the air;
Nine napkins needing a name;
Ten tambourines tinging and tanging.

— *Leroy, grade 4*

25 Windows

Description

This free-verse poem encourages children to use imagery and descriptive language. Brainstorm all the possible windows the children can think of and select the one that most inspires them. Have them imagine all the sights they can see from the window.

Lead-in Activity

On the chalkboard or overhead make two columns: "Windows" and "Views." Brainstorm different kinds of windows: stained glass, castle, tree house, lighthouse, train, airplane, White House, CN Tower, gondola, porthole, upstairs bedroom, and so on. Next, have children select their favorite five and brainstorm some things they might see from those windows. Using group consensus, choose one of the five from which to combine ideas into a group poem using the format suggested in the description. Read the following poems aloud, then have the children do individual poems and illustrate. The first and last lines of each poem read "From my [*adjective*] window I see…"

Windows Poem #1

From my tree house window, I can see
My friends and my parents all looking for me.
Their faces are in frowns and they call and shout.
I can see it getting dark and the moon is up.
I see my dog walking around in circles, wondering,
Wondering where I could possibly be.
The birds have all gone to bed and stopped chirping.
I'm getting very sleepy, too.
From my tree house window, I can see that
It's time for me to return to earth and go to bed!

— *Paloma, grade 4*

Windows Poem #2

From the rotating restaurant window
I can see the city of Buffalo below.
I can see Lake Erie and probably all the way to Pennsylvania.
I eat my cheeseburger and talk to my sister and then
I'm amazed to see that I see just the city
And it's getting dark and the lights go on.
The cars and buses rush around like
They have important places to go.
From the rotating restaurant window
Life goes fast but slow.

— *Brett, grade 4*

26 First Things First

(Adapted from First Things First *by Leland Jacobs)*

Description

This poetry style draws upon the use of comparisons, analogies, and simple sequences of events. It follows a unique structure that allows freedom of expression yet provides subtle direction to ensure writer success. The format is a three-line poem with the last line provided like so:

First the _____ and then the _____;
First the _____ and then the [*rhyme with above word*].
First things first.
First the _____ and then the _____;
First the _____ and then the [*rhyme with above word*].
First things first.
First the _____ and then the _____;
That's the way it had to be.
First things first.

Lead-in Activity

Read Leland Jacobs's poem *First Things First* (see page 149, appendix A) from which the format above was adapted. Allow children to discover that in this poem the last words in line one and two rhyme and that line seven rhymes with the word be. As a group, brainstorm things that usually happen in order and write them on the chalkboard. For example: "First the storm and then the rainbow"; "First the socks and then the shoes." When several lines have been brainstormed, have the children write a group poem using the format provided. Then read the example poems and have the children write poems individually or in pairs. Or, as an option, suggest to the children that they illustrate their sequence of items or activities by creating a border that starts with their first item in the lower, left-hand corner and goes clockwise around the page including every item or activity that has been mentioned.

First Things First #1

First you work and then you play;
You take out toys and then put them away.
First things first.
First you cook and then you eat;
You mess it up, then make it neat.
First things first.
First the homework, then the TV;
That's the way it had to be.
First things first.

— Vanessa, grade 3

First Things First #2

First the morning, then the night;
First the dark, then the bright.
First things first.
First you're young, then you're old;
First you're shy, then you're bold.
First things first.
First the river, then the sea;
That's the way it had to be.
First things first.

— LaTif, grade 3

27 This Old Man

Description

Using the rhythm of the familiar children's song, *This Old Man,* have the children write their own variation using the structure contained in the poetic verse. They may or may not choose to conform to the rhyme scheme.

Lead-in Activity

Write the words to *This Old Man* (see page 149, appendix A) on chart paper so that all can see them. Lead the children in singing the first verse of the song. Have the children decide upon actions to complement every line of the song. For example, for "This old man came rolling home," they can make a rolling motion with their hands. Provide the following format for children on the chart or chalkboard:

This [*adjective noun*]
He/she [*verb adjective*]
He/she [*verb noun prepositional phrase*].
With a [*one-syllable word one-syllable word two-syllable word one-syllable word*]
Give the [*subject*] a [*noun*],
This [*adjective subject*] came rolling home.

If the children are familiar with the parts of the speech indicated in the literacy scaffold, they may use them, but they will usually find it easier to merely sing the poem again to get an idea of what kind of word should come next, and deviation from the poem's format is acceptable in any case.

In small cooperative groups, have the children devise their own poem/song loosely fitting the "This Old Man" format. Encourage each group to share its original piece by singing or reciting it, and adding actions to accompany it. Allow groups to teach their new creation to the other children in the class.

This Pretty Piano (This Old Man Poem #1)

This pretty piano,
It plays good,
It plays high and very low notes
With a ding, dong, sing a song,
Give your note a tune,
This old piano came rolling soon.

— *Vicki, Jack, Dion, & Ray, grade 2*

This Fat Frog (This Old Man Poem #2)

This fat frog
He played dead.
He jumped far and lost his head
With a croak, croak, jumpy hop
Give the frog a fly.
This old frog came rolling by.

— *Rosco, Jennifer, Carmen, & Van, grade 2*

28 What Is Beautiful?

(Adapted from Poem of Praise *by Elizabeth Coatsworth)*

Description

This free-verse, two-stanza poem begins by painting a verbal picture of a beautiful thing using a series of descriptive phrases, and then goes on to illustrate that the opposite thing can also be beautiful. The contrast makes interesting poetry.

Lead-in Activity

Read the children *Poem of Praise* by Elizabeth Coatsworth (see page 149, appendix A). Have children make a list of things in nature that are swift and others that are slow. Generate another list of opposites that are found in nature, such as "large animals" and "small animals" or "animals that hatch from eggs" and "animals that are born live." Have groups of three or four children write their own poem using the format adapted from Coatsworth's poem:

First line: [*Adjective noun*] things are beautiful;
Middle line: And [*opposite*] are beautiful;

Old Things Are Beautiful (What Is Beautiful? #1)

Old things are beautiful;
   Big old oak trees
   That reach to the sky,
   Wise old owls
   That come out when
   It is very, very dark.
And young things are beautiful;
   Adorable baby kittens
   That don't even have their eyes open,
   Colts running in the pasture
   Their tails flying in the wind.

— Devon, grade 3

Quiet Things Are Beautiful (What Is Beautiful? #2)

Quiet things are beautiful;
   A gentle kind of rain
   That is dripping on my rooftop,
   Snow that falls in the mountains
   Covering every thing it sees
   With a peaceful white sound.
And loud things are beautiful;
   The marching band
   Leading the big parade,
   The crowd cheering
   When I hit my very first
   Home run.

— Brett, grade 4

29 When It Rains

Description

Here is an easy-to-write poem with no set number of lines that requires children to use their senses to articulate what happens when it rains. Every line begins with, "When it rains."

Lead-in Activity

Show children the wordless book *Rain* by Peter Spier and have them verbally recount the experiences of a rainy day as shown pictorially in the text.[2] Ask the children to brainstorm what happens to them, to the plants, and to all other living things when it rains. When all children who wish to have shared, write a group poem beginning each line with "When it rains." When the last person who wishes to has shared, create a last line, "And when it rains…" followed by a period. Read the group poem chorally and then encourage children to write their own "When It Rains" poem individually. To inspire children, distribute writing paper in the shape of an umbrella upon which they may write the final draft of their poems.

---

2. Peter Spier. *Rain.* New York: Doubleday, 1982.

When It Rains #1

When it rains there is lots of mud everywhere,
When it rains lightning can hit a tree.
When it rains all the flowers are happy.
When it rains puddles are born.
And when it rains even the sun gets wet.

— *Whitney, grade 2*

When It Rains #2

When it rains God is crying
Because he doesn't like something we did.
When it rains the sun is gone
From the sky and from people's faces,
When it rains we have to stay inside
And people get sleepy and sometimes grumpy,
I really don't like, not even a little bit,
When it rains.

— *Hector, grade 3*

Part II

Intermediate Scaffolds

Clerihews

Description

In these poems, students pick a famous person and write a humorous (or serious) synopsis of that person's life, using a simple *a-a-b-b* format. The last name of the chosen person is the impetus for the rhyme. Alternatively, the format can be used for mini-biographies or mini-autobiographies of children in the class.

Lead-in Activity

To introduce the concept of rhyming phrases that encapsulate a person's characteristics or habitual actions, read the following couplets aloud. Then have children brainstorm ways to complete the following clerihews, after reading the first two examples:

1. Axl Rose, moves on his toes.
2. Alexander Graham Bell, I can hear you so well.
3. Minnie Mouse, _____.
4. Martin Luther King, _____.

Finally, have the students write their own poems. They can refer to these sample poems to guide them:

Edgar Allan Poe (Clerihew #1)

Edgar Allan Poe,
You do scare me so!
I bite all my nails,
While reading your tales.

— Kalisa, grade 3

Janet Brown (Clerihew #2)
(Mini-biography)

Janet Brown,
You never seem to frown.
All the while,
I just see you smile.

— Tessa, grade 3

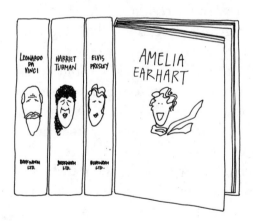

2 Fifteen Words

Description

This "instant" poem is a sure hit with those youngsters who are certain that they cannot write poetry. Additionally, the format provides an opportunity for children to appreciate figurative and connotative language. Children are asked to make a list of their fifteen favorite words, which can come from any resource available to them. They are then given a blank poem format (see Lead-in Activity) and asked to arrange their words in the manner that they feel is the most appealing.

Lead-in Activity

Discuss favorite words. Ask the children if they have favorite words. Share *your* favorite words and tell why you like them. Without letting children know why they are doing it, ask them to write down fifteen of their favorite words. These words can be names, food, places, or they might be selected for their sound (*pumpernickel*) or their positive association (*birthday*). Words can be from another language for those children who know one. Words needn't be related to one another. As children are thinking about their words, encourage them to walk around the room and read their classmates' words and perhaps borrow some of those if they wish. When all the students have a list of fifteen words, read the following poems aloud. Then ask the students to create a poem using the following format, experimenting freely with different combinations, adding articles (*a, an, the*) or prepositions (*onto, near,* and so on) as needed, and throwing out words that they no longer want:

———— ————,
———— ———— ————.
———— ————,
————.
———— ———— ———— ————,
————,
———— ————.

When the children are finished writing their poems, encourage them to read them to one another in small groups. (Sometimes older children enjoy looking for hidden "psychological" meanings in the poems.)

Geronimo (Fifteen Words Poem #1)

Jumbo pony,
Fanciful, gentle flower.
Cinderella pickles,
Pow!
Pumpernickel jeepers, holy wow,
Geronimo!
I'm cool!

— Jemma, grade 4

Adios Animals (Fifteen Words Poem #2)

Adios animals,
Humongous babbling brook,
Hidey ho,
Octopus.
Tacos on hot sizzlers.
Awesome!
Amazing chrysanthemum.

— Raúl, grade 5

3 Biopoetry

Description

Biopoetry is a short, ten-line biography that tells certain prescribed facts about the life of a person. The format is especially useful in conjunction with a social studies unit on a world leader, explorer, or inventory, or as an activity to extend a biography that children have read. Use the following pattern:

Line 1: [*First name only*] _____ .
Line 2: [*Four traits*] _____ .
Line 3: Related to _____ .
Line 4: Cares deeply about _____ .
Line 5: Who feels _____ .
Line 6: Who needs _____ .
Line 7: Who gives _____ .
Line 8: Who fears _____ .
Line 9: Who would like to see _____ .
Line 10: Resident of _____ .

Lead-in Activity

Discuss with children the word *biography*. Ask them to name biographies they have read. Next, list on the chalk-board or overhead, with children's input, all the character-istics of a person's life that are generally contained in a biography. Select a favorite fairy tale character such as Cinderella or Yeh Shen. Ask the children to name features that they feel might be included in a biography of that character. Brainstorm some other fictional, currently famous, or cartoon characters about whom children might like to write biopoetry. Before having the children write their own biopoetry, read the following poems aloud. (Provide copies of the format for the poem.)

Peter Pan (Biopoetry #1)

Peter.
Young, lively, mischievous, brave.
Friend of the lost boys.
Cares deeply about Wendy.
Who feels like a little boy.
Who needs a mother.
Who gives flying lessons.
Who fears growing up.
Who would like to see Wendy again.
Resident of Never Never Land.

— *Ali, grade 3*

My Teacher (Biopoetry #2)

Mrs. Rodriguez.
Smart, kind, caring, organized.
Related to Mr. Rodriguez.
Cares deeply about her students' minds.
Who feels responsible for her class.
Who needs to teach children.
Who gives out scratch 'n' sniff stickers.
Who fears a teachers' strike.
Who would like to see all her students promoted
    to sixth grade.
Resident of P.S. Number 40.

— *Rhonda, grade 5*

4 I Meant to…

(Adapted from I Meant to Clean My Room Today *by Miriam Nerlove)*

Description

This poem provides an easy-to-use seven-line literacy scaffold through which children can describe a time when they put off doing something they were supposed to do in favor of doing something they would rather do—a universal theme for children (and adults). The format is as follows:

I meant to _____ today,
But _____ ,
And _____ ,
And _____ ,
And _____ .
I meant to _____ today,
But _____ got in my way.

Lead-in Activity

Write the word *procrastination* on the chalkboard or overhead. Discuss this word with children and ask them if they have ever put off doing some chore or activity that they were supposed to do. Give examples of when *you* have procrastinated (to demonstrate that it is a "human" phenomenon). Brainstorm some activities that the children have put off doing and make a list of them. Read the book *I Meant to Clean My Room Today* by Miriam Nerlove.[3] After reading the following poems, give children the skeleton provided in the description and have them write their own poems.

---

3. Miriam Nerlove. *I Meant to Clean My Room Today.* New York: M.K. McElderry Books, 1988.

I Meant to Go On a Diet (I Meant to Poem #1)

I meant to go on a diet today,
But that lonely toast at breakfast was needing some jelly,
And everyone wanted to go to McDonald's for lunch,
And Hoá insisted on sharing her french fries with me,
And there was a caramel flan for dessert after dinner.
I meant to go on a diet today,
But food got in my way!

— LaToya, grade 6

I Meant to Do My Homework (I Meant to Poem #2)

I meant to do my homework today.
But all the neighbor kids were playing in the street,
And then my big brother wanted to play Nintendo,
And then there was a scary movie on TV,
And then I fell asleep immediately after I opened
    my math book.
I meant to do my homework today,
But other more fun things got in my way!

— Jared, grade 5

Sneakers
(Tiedt & Tiedt 1987)

Description

In this five-line, unrhymed poem, the topic is revealed slowly, not coming to light until the last line (thus "sneaking up" on the reader).

The specific format is as follows:

Line 1: [*Noun related to subject*].
Line 2: [*Adjective and noun related to the subject*].
Line 3: [*Two action words related to the subject*].
Line 4: [*Phrase describing the subject*].
Line 5: [*Subject revealed*].

Lead-in Activity

To prepare children for the subtle descriptive element of this poem, have children play a guessing game. Place a common object, such as a pair of scissors, in a paper bag. Without naming the object, describe its function, physical characteristics, and importance. Have children guess what the object might be and ask them to explain their guesses. Give several children in the class an opportunity to similarly select an object and slowly describe it without revealing its identity while the other children try to guess what it is. When all who wish to have played the guessing game, do a group poem with children using the format provided in the description. Then brainstorm some other objects that might be used for individual poems. After reading example poems, have the children write their own sneakers.

Pen (Sneakers Poem #1)

Utensil.
Sleek object.
Writing, composing.
Putting thoughts onto paper for you.
Pen.

— *Arturo, grade 5*

Television (Sneakers Poem #2)

Amusement.
Colorful machine.
Entertaining, informing.
Almost everybody I know has one.
Television.

— *Jennifer, grade 5*

6 Symmetrical Bios

Description

These poems enhance self-esteem and promote students' appreciation for one another. This type of poem has several unique characteristics: it is symmetrical in its linear format, it contains phrases about the personal traits of the person for whom it is written, and each line begins with a letter from that person's name. For example, take a poem about someone whose name is David. It would contain five lines, each describing personal traits of David. The first letter of the first word in the first line would begin with *D,* the first letter of the second word in the second line with *A,* and so forth. The poem is symmetrical—each line must contain a certain number of words so that when the poem is divided into two parts, each contains the same number of words. To be symmetrical, the poem might have two words in the first line, four words in the second line, five words in the third line, four words in the fourth line, and two words in the last line. Other symmetrical possibilities are:

D	3 words in first line.		*D*	1 word in first line.
A	5 words in second line.		*A*	4 words in second line.
V	1 word in third line.		*V*	6 words in third line.
I	5 words in fourth line.		*I*	4 words in fourth line.
D	3 words in fifth line.		*D*	1 word in fifth line.

Lead-in Activity

Write the word *symmetry* on the chalkboard or overhead. Using a picture or rough line drawing of a butterfly, demonstrate that the butterfly's wings are symmetrical; in other words, if she were to be divided in half, each side would be identical. Explain to the children that they will be writing a symmetrical biography of a classmate. Each line will begin with a letter of the classmate's first name, and the lines must be symmetrical; that is, the placement of words in the top half must be identical to the placement of words in the bottom half of the poem. Use the name of a famous person (for example, Abraham) to show how this is done. Show various symmetrical patterns that could be used. Also, read the example poems aloud and help children to point out the symmetrical scheme used. Ask each child to select a partner (triads can also be used) for whom they will write a symmetrical bio poem. Instruct children that any interesting information can be used, but it must all be "good" and "true"; do not use physical traits.

Karen (Symmetrical Bio Poem #1)

K nows lots about animals, (4)
A very good artist, too. (5)
R eally likes to make new friends (6)
E ven though she is shy. (5)
N ever has a frown! (4)

— Ramona, grade 6

Anne (Symmetrical Bio Poem #2)

A really fine Nintendo player, (5)
N ever is without answers in class, (6)
N obody likes her more than me, (6)
E veryone can see she's kind! (5)

— Tess, grade 5

7 Diners

(Adapted from The Diners in the Kitchen *by James Whitcomb Riley)*

Description

This seven couplet literacy scaffold, adapted from James Whitcomb Riley's *The Diners in the Kitchen,* is an excellent introduction for children to one of America's great poets:

Our dog _____,
Ate the _____.
Our dog _____,
Ate the _____.
Our dog _____,
Ate the _____.
Our dog _____,
Ate the _____.
Our dog _____,
Ate the _____.
And—the worst
From the first—
Our dog _____,
Ate the _____.

Lead-in Activity

Ask for a show of hands of children who have or have had pets. Write the names of their pets on the chalkboard or overhead as they offer them. For each animal name, brainstorm a rhyming word that is also a food. For example: *Fido, potato* and *Lucille, veal.* Tell them that the rhyme need not be exact and that they may change the food a bit to "force" the rhyme, as in *Fifi, beefy.* Read aloud the poem *The Diners in the Kitchen* (see page 150, appendix A) and the students' poems. Give children copies of the scaffold above and have them write their own "Diners" poem.

Diners Poem #1

Our dog Hillary,
Ate the celery.
Our dog Rasta,
Ate the pasta.
Our dog Willie,
Ate the chili.
Our dog Tip,
Ate the onion dip.
Our dog Lola,
Drank the cola.
And—the worst
From the first—
Our dog Donkey,
Ate the turkey.

    — Rosa, grade 3

Diners Poem #2

Our dog Gopher,
Ate the meat loafer.
Our dog Falana,
Ate the banana.
Our dog Fufu,
Ate the tofu.
Our dog Gushi,
Ate the sushi.
Our dog Ben,
Ate the game hen.
And—the worst
From the first—
Our dog Jake,
Ate the cake.

    — Raphael, grade 3

8 Diamante

Description

Using only seven lines, this formula poem describes a specific subject using prescribed parts of speech in the following format:

Line 1: [*Subject*]
Line 2: [*Two adjectives describing the subject*]
Line 3: [*Three participles (words ending in* ing) *telling about the subject*]
Line 4: [*Four words, two of which describe the subject and two of which are the opposite of the subject*]
Line 5: [*Three participles that are the opposite of the subject*]
Line 6: [*Two adjectives that are opposite of the subject*]
Line 7: [*One noun that is the opposite of the subject*]

This format creates a diamond shape; it is one of a number of formats for what are known as "shape poems."

Lead-in Activity

Review with the children the concept of a noun and make a list of nouns on the chalkboard or overhead. Suggest that nouns, such as *love, war, tornado, greed,* and so on, can also represent intangible items. List intangible nouns under separate headings. For each of the intangible items, ask children if they can think of a word opposite to the intangible word (for example, love/hate, war/peace, greed/generosity, and so on). Explain to children that they are going to write a poem about one of these nouns—either tangible or intangible—first describing the item and then describing the opposite of the item they chose. Read the following poems aloud and then write a group diamante about an item chosen by group consensus. Then invite children to choose their own item and write individual diamantes. (Diamantes are also fun for children to write in small cooperative groups.)

War (Diamante Poem #1)

War
Bloody, deadly
Fighting, killing, bombing
Destruction, devastation, harmony, unity
Collaborating, cooperating, helping
Serene, calm
Peace

— *Adak, grade 5*

Dog (Diamante Poem #2)

Dog
Loyal, faithful
Barking, growling, whining
Guarding, protecting, licking, napping
Mewing, purring, clawing
Independent, shy
Cat

— *Zachary, grade 5*

9 Haiku

Description

This poetic form, which originated in Japan in the thirteenth century, is used to express an observation about a season or some aspect of nature. For children who have already had some experience with less difficult scaffolds, this format can be an enjoyable way for them to write a succinct poem about *any* topic—not just nature. Using this format, children write a three-line verse concentrating on a single visual or auditory image. By crossing out unnecessary words they can make their poem into the required 5-7-5 syllabic pattern, although for beginning poets the syllable count need not be strictly adhered to. The standard haiku format is as follows:

Line 1: [*What or who*] (5 syllables)
Line 2: [*Feeling, action, or description*] (7 syllables)
Line 3: [*A summative phrase*] (5 syllables)

Lead-in Activity

Have children brainstorm favorite seasons and/or elements in nature such as snow, a rainbow, thunder, or wind. For each topic, find appropriate words or phrases that come to children's minds. Write a group haiku. Next, have children use the following art activity to help them crystallize their feelings about a chosen topic.

Cut along the sides of small brown paper bags, crumble them, and immerse them in hot water. Then cut off 4 in. by 6 in. (10 cm x 15 cm) rectangles from the bags and lay flat. When the paper is dry, iron to flatten, and tear the edges. Glue onto the upper half of a piece of white construction paper. With straws and tempera paint, have children depict their topic on the bottom of the white construction paper. Encourage them to write their own haiku to correspond to the feelings expressed in their tempera scene. Their haiku can then be written with black felt-tipped marker on the top of the brown paper.

Thunder (Haiku #1)

Drums beating in the sky
Trying to scare all the birds
A storm is coming.

— Jenny, grade 5

Fog (Haiku #2)

Clouds all around me;
No one can see anything.
Little tiny rain.

— Jamal, grade 6

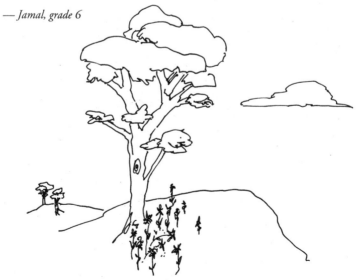

10 Found Phrases

Description

Found phrases poems are made up of words and phrases that are culled from—or "found" in—the environment. Using books, magazines, posters, and newspapers, children find headlines, slogans, mottoes, and other interesting words to arrange in a unique setting to suggest a new meaning or to emphasize unusual sounds.

Lead-in Activity

Give students specific ideas of where to look for interesting, content-laden words and phrases (for example, newspaper headlines, posters, magazine articles, manuals, highway signs, and even miscellaneous signs around the school building). Give them a deadline to "collect" twenty or so such words and phrases. Next, read the following poems aloud, then have the children share the words and phrases they have found and, as a group, make a poem out of ordinary, everyday words and phrases that have been arranged in a new way. Finally, invite children to create their own found phrases poems.

Specific Questions (Found Phrases Poem #1)

Important memo
Warm air
Truck to its fleet
Asking for contributions
Senate passed
Ultra-clean fuel
Without the hassle
Only sixty calories a slice
Women invited to apply
High road
Specific questions are raised

— Hilda, grade 7

Grass Fire (Found Phrases Poem #2)

Grass fire,
Arsonist suspected.
Cheesy taste.
Unemployment figures
Conveniently available.
Exceptional value.
Looking for something different?
Stimulate the economy.
A Wild West Journey
To the edge of time.

— Cassandra, grade 8

11 Animal Alphabets

Description

This poem has twenty-six lines, one for every letter of the alphabet. The first letter of the first line in the verse is *A,* the first letter of the second line is *B,* and so on through the alphabet. The verse names 104 animals, birds, fishes, or insects and is arranged in simple rhyming couplets.

Lead-in Activity

Write the names of four classes of animals on the chalkboard or overhead: mammals, birds, fish, and insects. As a group, brainstorm items for each category. When children can think of no more, divide the class into four groups according to the categories. Using the encyclopedia, dictionary, and resources such as *Ranger Rick, Owl Magazine,* and *National Geographic's World,* have children compile as many items as they can to complete the columns. Then read the two example poems aloud, pointing out the rhyming, couplets, and the initial animal corresponding to the letter of the alphabet. Have children brainstorm other rhyming animals to use in poems. Group the children in twos or threes and have them write their own animal alphabet poems.

Animal Alphabet #1

Anteater, marmoset, chipmunk, cub,
Beaver, rooster, armadillo, grub.
Coyote, puffer, condor, bear,
Diamondback, parrotfish, pelican, hare.
Elephant, firefly, dragonfly, lobster,
Ferret, crayfish, swallow, hamster.
Golden eagle, muskrat, cricket, moth,
Hyena, gorilla, starfish, sloth.
Iguana, cottontail, catbird, shark,
Javelina, mountain goat, bobcat, lark.
King snake, salamander, crocodile, mole,
Lion, koala bear, beaver, tadpole.
Mink, hippopotamus, turtle, kangaroo,
Napir, caribou, crane, cockatoo.
Ostrich, reindeer, buffalo, dog,
Panda, loris, German shepherd, hog.
Quail, weasel, rattlesnake, eel,
Rhinoceros, tortoise, cat, cockatiel.
Scorpion, python, nuthatch, crow,
Termite, lion, turkey, armadillo.
Unicorn, silverfish, caterpillar, fox,
Vole, spider, giraffe, ox.
Waterbug, grebe, lingcod, bat,
Xeme, lemur, otter, rat.
Yellowbird, hornet, walrus, goose,
Zebra, snoutfish, woodpecker, moose.

— Ramón, grade 6

Animal Alphabet #2

Aardvark, cardinal, dingo, frog,
Badger, camel, clownfish, hog.
Caterpillar, crayfish, lizard, manta ray,
Dinosaur, pheasant, wolf, aye-aye.
Earthworm, python, scallop, flea,
Filefish, mongoose, porpoise, bee.
Groundhog, leopard, prairie dog, snail,
Halibut, monkey, mouse, blue-nosed whale.
Impala, pigeon, raccoon, owl,
Jaguar, dolphin, penguin, fowl.
Kiwi, oriole, orangutan, loon,
Lemming, protozoa, harp seal, baboon.
Mosquito, peacock, puffin, hamster,
Nuthatch, hummingbird, heron, gopher.
Octopus, killdeer, guinea pig, lobster,
Peacock, osprey, rabbit, grouper.
Quail, robin, merlin, sparrow,
Raccoon, lemur, drumfish, minnow.
Shark, turkey, woodchuck, swan,
Thrush, weasel, snoutfish, fawn.
Unicorn, collie, poodle, magpie,
Vole, sea slug, chameleon, dragonfly.
Wasp, brown recluse, skunk, wolverine,
Xeme, lynx, puma, nene.
Yellow-bellied trout, worm, parakeet, peregrine,
Zebra, lemming, dormouse, ermine.

— Sasha, grade 5

12 Name Alphabets

Description

Like Animal Alphabet, this poem format has twenty-six lines, one for every letter of the alphabet. The first letter of the first line in the verse is *A,* the first letter of the second line is *B,* and so on through the poem. The poem consists entirely of names. The poem is composed in simple rhyming couplets: *a-a-b-b-c-c* and so on.

Lead-in Activity

Write the first names of all the children in the class on the chalkboard or overhead. Ask children to come up and join two names if they rhyme. For names that have no rhyming partners, brainstorm first names they have heard that rhyme with these names. Made-up names are acceptable if no "legitimate" rhyme can be found. Read the two example poems aloud, pointing out the rhyming couplets. Then have the children write their own name alphabet poems.

Name Alphabet #1

Alexander, Hoa, Jamál, Christine,
Barbara, Dion, José, Irene.
Charles, Nabil, Azadek, John,
David, Mao, Kimberly, Don.
Ellen, Raúl, Janice, Mickey,
Franco, Hillary, Jennifer, Nicky.
Graciela, Tiffani, Ryan, Penny,
Hannah, Miguel, Ricardo, Benny.
Isabella, Heffa, Cristobal, Juan,
Jackie, Roberto, Marianne, Tán.
Kevin, Sheila, Tamara, Judy,
Linda, Peter, Komodo, Rudy.
Mehán, Laura, Christopher, Jan,
Nancy, Gloria, Tabitha, San.
Octavia, Sharon, Boris, Kate,
Paulo, Carlos, Fernando, Nate.
Quito, Arthur, Cindy, Brett,
Robert, Amy, Kieran, Rhett.
Svetlana, William, Ida, Sandy,
Teresa, Andrew, Reginald, Randy.
Uta, Brandi, Vera, Ray,
Velma, Teddy, Habib, Jay.
Warren, Daniel, Iraj, Pat,
Xavier, Mehran, Gary, Matt.
Yetta, Harry, Dianna, Sam,
Zelda, Ali, Kathy, Pam.

— Svetlana, grade 5

Name Alphabet #2

Abigail, Kristen, Tracey, Jill,
Bobby, Monica, Winnie, Bill.
Catherine, Dina, Justine, Dolly,
Damien, Marcus, Opal, Molly.
Edgar, Mary, Maria, Mary Lou,
Fernando, Teija, Carrie, Betty Sue.
Gena, Sergio, Susan, Joe,
Hilda, Danielle, Robin, Chloe.
Ilsa, Tony, Mark, Stu,
Juanita, Laurence, Marilyn, Hugh.
Kelly, Michael, Helena, Rob,
Luanna, Deborah, Jeffrey, Bob.
Magic, Whitney, Natassja, Lyndie,
Nicole, Blair, Jonathan, Cindy.
Oprah, Gerri, José, Tim,
Pablo, Thomas, Julio, Jim.
Quinn, Elvis, Mandy, Sean,
Roxanne, Emily, Griffin, Fawn.
Shannon, Allen, Brandon, Will,
Tyler, Alvin, LaToya, Gill.
Uguri, Brenda, Tisha, Bart,
Vincent, Buffy, Suki, Art.
Wilma, Karen, Brittany, Ken,
Xerxes, Nadia, Steven, Len.
Yolanda, Howard, Ariel, Anne,
Zuki, Freda, Larry, Jan.

— *Juanita, grade 6*

Place Alphabets

Description

Much like Animal Alphabet and Name Alphabet in format, this poem has a geographic focus. There are twenty-six lines, one for every letter of the alphabet. The first letter of the first line in the verse must be *A;* the first letter of the second line must be *B,* and so on throughout the poem. The words of the poem consist of places in the world. The poem is in simply rhyming couplets.

Lead-in Activity

Using maps and globes, have the children name the continents. Write these in one column on the chalkboard or overhead. Then choose a volunteer to select a country. Challenge the other children to name another country that rhymes with or has the same ending sound as that country. Use the same procedure with states, provinces, and cities. When a wide selection of rhyming states, provinces, cities, and countries has been compiled, explain to the class that they will be writing poems that are made up of places in the world and that they can use the rhyming words on the chalkboard to help them with their poems. Read example poems to illustrate. Have the children work in groups of two or three, using a globe or map if necessary.

Place Alphabet #1

Africa, Oklahoma, Bogota, Oslo,
Boise, Alabama, Denver, Idaho.
Chicago, Chile, Wyoming, Alaska,
Detroit, Pennsylvania, West Virginia, North Dakota.
Edinburgh, Israel, Egypt, Rome,
France, Nigeria, Dallas, Nome.
Ghana, Siberia, Somalia, Glasgow,
Harrisburg, Auckland, Lima, Moscow.
Iowa, Pittsburgh, Germany, Italy,
Jacksonville, Tampa, New Orleans, Sicily.
Kansas, Hong Kong, Boston, Singapore,
Lagos, Juneau, Seattle, Baltimore.
Miami, Helsinki, South Dakota, Lucerne,
Nairobi, Texas, Connecticut, Bern.
Ottawa, Orlando, Florida, Spain,
Philadelphia, Paris, Indiana, Ukraine.
Quito, Scotland, Colombia, Norway,
Rhode Island, Albuquerque, Arizona, Bombay.
St. Louis, Georgia, Madagascar, Maine,
Thailand, Nebraska, Cincinnati, Brisbane.
Uruguay, Santa Fe, Fairbanks, Fort Worth,
Virginia, Montana, Ohio, Perth.
Waikiki, Havana, Puerto Rico, Mexico,
Xenia, Alberta, Missouri, Buffalo.
Yucatán, Taiwan, Japan, Tokyo,
Zurich, Belgrade, Iceland, Cairo.

— *Micah, grade 5*

Place Alphabet #2

Altoona, Botswana, Wisconsin, Spain,
Budapest, California, Washington, Maine.
Chattanooga, Fiji, Nevada, Chapel Hill,
Denver, Oklahoma, Massachusetts, Brazil.
England, Iceland, Greenland, Oslo,
Frankfurt, Davenport, Freeport, Idaho.
Greece, Turkey, Oklahoma, Tennessee,
Hawaii, Kansas City, Virgin Islands, Wounded Knee.
Indiana, Sweden, Belgium, South Bend,
Juneau, Mississippi, Sacramento, Land's End.
Kenya, Liberia, France, Kalamazoo,
Lima, China, Switzerland, Peru.
Mozambique, Trinidad, New York, Chad,
Newark, Delaware, Athens, Baghdad.
Orlando, Laramie, Brussels, Cheyenne,
Peoria, Madras, Portland, Japan.
Quebec, Montreal, Canada, Hilo,
Richmond, San Diego, Reno, Ohio.
San Francisco, Guatemala, Las Vegas, Katmandu,
Tunisia, Albania, Alabama, Timbuktu.
Utah, London, Paris, Manhattan,
Venezuela, Argentina, Cleveland, Wisconsin.
Walla Walla, Hong Kong, Krakow, Samoa,
Xenia, Madrid, Chicago, Balboa.
Youngstown, Akron, Geneva, Iran,
Zanzibar, Leningrad, Maui, Pakistan.

— Miriam, grade 6

14 Limericks

Description

Children enjoy these humorous structured poems if they
have had enough background in free verse to be able to
"play" with the flexible rhyme scheme. The poem tells a
fanciful, amusing tale about a character, usually a person
or animal. The format consists of a triplet and a couplet in
an *a-a-b-b-a* arrangement.

Lead-in Activity

Read the example limericks to the children. Explain that
limericks are usually written about everyday people doing
ordinary things. Ask children why limericks are so funny.
Show the children the rhyme scheme, and how it allows
the reader to look at a mundane experience in a fresh,
humorous way. Before the children write their own limericks, do a group limerick. Offer an opening such as:
"There was a young farmer from Kent…" or "There was a
shy lady from Stowe…," then ask the children for suggestions. Select one as the first line for a group limerick.
Guide children to adapt their ideas to the rhyme scheme
as they offer line suggestions. If a line does *not* fit the
scheme, have other children help to modify the words so
that the line *does* fit the rhyme scheme without changing
the contributor's original ideas. When children have
finished, read the group limerick, exaggerating the rhythm
of the rhyme scheme. Finally, encourage children to write
individual limericks using one of the beginning lines
brainstormed in class or another of their own creation.

Limerick #1

There was a cute puppy named Joe,
Who liked to chase anything slow.
He'd follow a snail,
While wagging his tail,
And be passed by six cats in a row!

— *Vladimir, grade 6*

Limerick #2

There was a young fellow from Galt,
Whose rap group was named Pepper & Salt.
His lyrics were bad,
So his parents got mad,
But he said that it wasn't his fault.

— *Boris, grade 6*

Cinquains

Description

The cinquain is a traditional poem consisting of five lines in the following prescribed format:

Line 1: [*One word—the title*]
Line 2: [*Two words describing the title*]
Line 3: [*Three words—actions describing the title*]
Line 4: [*Four participles, or* ing *words, about the title*]
Line 5: [*One word that summarizes the title*]

An alternative form of the cinquain concerns itself with numbers of syllables rather than specific parts of speech. This is one possibility:

Line 1: [*Two syllables*]
Line 2: [*Four syllables*]
Line 3: [*Six syllables*]
Line 4: [*Eight syllables*]
Line 5: [*Two syllables*]

Lead-in Activity

The cinquain, in either of the formats described above, is ideally suited to topics from the content areas of science or social studies. Using cinquains, the children can summarize key ideas in a particular unit of study. After a unit on whales, for example, have children brainstorm some of the key ideas they remember, using specific words and phrases. To crystallize their thinking on the topic they can cut out pictures from newspapers and magazines and organize them into a topic collage. Then, after being shown the cinquain format, children can write their own cinquains about the topic. Read the following examples aloud to show the pattern:

Cinquain #1

Whales
Large creatures.
Swim, dive, splash.
Spouting, eating, mating, migrating.
Mammals.

— Vivian, grade 6

Cinquain #2

King
Noble man.
Lived, thought, marched, cared.
Believing, dreaming, preaching, changing.
Hero.

— Dion, grade 6

16 Free Verse

Description

This free verse contains virtually no restrictions as to pattern of rhyme, length of line, or topic and, for that reason, is more open than more rigidly prescribed rhyme schemes. Have children use this format to simply "tell an idea."

Lead-in Activity

To make this ambiguous poetic format accessible to all students, show them a slide or picture about an event or other happening. Have the students contribute words or phrases that describe the ideas in the picture or how the picture makes them feel. Write these on the chalkboard or overhead in free-verse format, illustrating the capitalization of each line and the simplicity of the format. Provide the children with other pictures or slides to inspire their own free-verse poem. Read example poems.

In the Park (Free Verse #1)

Boys playing in the park
Laughing at nothing and throwing a ball.
They look so happy.
They must all be best friends.
The leaves fall around them in many colors.
It must be autumn in the park.

— Vanna, grade 5

Jennie's Present (Free Verse #2)

A feeling so bright and cheerful!
The girl looks like my friend Jennie.
Jennie opens a huge, beautifully wrapped present.
Is it your birthday, Jennie?
I guess that it must be.
You look so glad, it must be your special day.
I hope you get the new doll that you want!

— Maria, grade 5

17 Answers

Description
This free-verse poem allows children to reflect upon important feelings that they have and then express those feelings into verse.

Lead-in Activity
Tell children you are going to ask them how they feel about five things, and that you want them to answer in phrases or short sentences. Explain that they do not have to share their responses, and that there are no right or wrong answers. When they have answered the questions, encourage them to rearrange their answers, add any words that they feel are necessary, and experiment with word placements until they have a recognizable poem that expresses their feelings. Use some of the following queries (or any others you can think of) to inspire "poetic" responses. The answers to these questions form the basis for the poem:

What does the word *friendship* mean to you?
What are some characteristics of your best friend?
Why do you like him or her?
What is your favorite season of the year? Why?
What kinds of things do you do in that season?
What appeals to you about those things?
Summarize your feelings today.

You may want to read the following poems aloud before the students write their own poems.

Answers Poem #1

Loyalty, caring, sharing, being silly together.
Kind, a great listener, really fun to be with.
Spring!
All things I couldn't do in winter.
Walking in the rain, avoiding puddles, glad to see the sun.
I feel really terrific!

— Sal, grade 5

Answers Poem #2

Someone's always there to talk to.
Funny, kind, helpful, really smart.
My friend is always there for me.
In the cold, snowy winter
I don't have to feel bad I'm not a jock.
I huddle in the house by the fire reading a book
Or playing Nintendo with my friend.
I'm in the best mood in a long, long time.

— John, grade 6

18 Lanterne

Description

When completed, this five-line, eleven-syllable shape poem takes the form of a Japanese lantern. The pattern is as follows:

Line 1: [*One syllable, usually the topic and a noun*]
Line 2: [*Two syllables about the topic*]
Line 3: [*Three syllables about the topic*]
Line 4: [*Four syllables about the topic*]
Line 5: [*One syllable—a reaction to the topic*]

Lead-in Activity

Write the examples on the chalkboard or overhead, then read them aloud, pointing out the special visual feature and explaining the pattern. Brainstorm with the children about topics such as months, seasons, holidays, major events, or specific weather phenomena, writing down all their ideas. Use these words and phrases to write a group lanterne, then encourage children to select another topic and write their own lanterne poem, either individually or in pairs. Have them paste their finished poems on brightly colored construction paper shaped like lanterns.

Lanterne #1

March.
Blowing
Kites, hair, clouds
Rainy, windy,
Whoosh!

— *Peter, grade 6*

Lanterne #2

Cake
Mixing
Eggs, flour, spice
Bake in oven.
Yum!

— *Rachel, grade 5*

19 Arguments

Description

This scaffold is an excellent device through which children can cope with strong feelings about a particular topic. A free-verse poem, the format provides six or more reasons either for or against something; the last reason being the strongest argument. Each line provides a different argument for or against the topic.

Lead-in Activity

Divide the class into two groups. Have one group respond positively to the idea of owning a boa constrictor and provide at least six reasons for snake ownership. Have the other group respond negatively, coming up with at least six reasons why owning a boa constrictor would be a bad idea. Then write each group's ideas into two separate argument poems, connecting their reasons for or against with "because" as shown in the examples. Then, with the entire group, brainstorm several other issues about which children might have strong "for" or "against" feelings, such as eating meat, going to school, going bungee jumping, getting their ears pierced, and so on.

Pierced Ears (Argument Poem #1)

I really want to get my ears pierced
Because my earrings wouldn't get lost anymore
And because I think they look cool
And because it's a grown-up thing to do
And because sometimes even babies have them
And because pierced earrings are nicer than clip-ons,
And because my mother promised maybe when I was ten,
And mostly because Maria and Cindi have them.

— *Chrissy, grade 4*

Don't Smoke (Argument Poem #2)

People should not ever smoke
Because it makes their lungs get all black
And because it causes air pollution
And because some people are allergic to smoke
And because it makes your hands smell gross
And because you cough all the time
And because smoking gives you more colds
And mostly because lung cancer can kill you.

— *Kristen, grade 5*

20 Love Songs

Description

In this free-verse ode, the poets get to profess their undying love (tongue-in-cheek) for a common object they like.

Lead-in Activity

Define the word *ode* to the children. (An ode is a lofty poem addressed to a person or thing.) Ask them if they know any love songs. Invite them to share the words of any they know. Discuss why they think the writer has penned a love song. Ask children if they think they could write a humorous love song to a common object such as a pencil or animal such as a dog. Read children the humorous ode *Love Song for a Jellyfish* by Sandra Hochman (see page 150, appendix A.) Then have them brainstorm some similar animals or objects that would be fun to write about. Ask them to select one animal or object and write a love song to it after listening to the examples. Objects can include a can opener, the rain, a window, a tonsil, a sneaker, a baseball cap, and so on.

Rain (Love Song #1)

Oh, rain on my windowpane!
You have made all the flowers grow
And created huge puddles for me to splash in
And jump over.
You come down wetly on my new red umbrella
Making little plinking sounds that make me laugh.
I love you so and want you to know, though,
That if you go away tomorrow
And the sun is shining instead
I will quickly forget all about you!

— Randy, grade 5

Pockets (Love Song #2)

Oh, pockets in my favorite, most comfortable jeans!
You have been so kind to my money and all my stuff.
Whenever my hand goes near you
I feel better just knowing you are taking care of
    everything for me.
I just love your wide, roomy, accepting nature!
You carry my load, but you never complain.
One of these days, out of love for you, I will
Remove your contents and give you peace.

— Cyrus, grade 6

21 Grammar Poems

Description

Because this poetic format tells the poet exactly what to do, the scaffold allows anyone to write a satisfying, well-constructed poem simply by filling in the parts of speech as required. The format is as follows:

[Title—Noun/s]

[*Noun*],
[*Noun*],
[*Noun*].
[*Adjective noun*],
[*Adjective noun*].
[*Adjective, adjective, adjective noun*].
[*Adjective, adjective, adjective noun*].
Those are just a few.
[*Adjective noun*],
[*Adjective noun*],
[*Participle, participle, participle noun*].
[*Participle, participle, participle noun*].
[*Adjective noun*], too.
[*Adjective noun*],
[*Adjective noun*],
[*Adjective noun*].
Don't forget [*adjective noun*].
Last of all—best of all—
I like [*adjective noun*].

Lead-in Activity

Review adjectives, nouns, and participles. Tell the children they can write interesting poems using sixteen adjectives and six participles that describe a person, place, or thing of their choice. Read the two example poems. Have the children select a topic. Brainstorm sixteen adjectives and six participles that describe the topic. Have children put the words in the proper category. Next, brainstorm several new topics, such as bees, trees, cookies, brothers, babies, and shoes. Divide the class into groups of three to write poems or let them write their own poems, providing copies of a blank scaffold or using the overhead or chalkboard to illustrate.

Babies (Grammar Poem #1)

Babies,
Babies,
Babies.
Big babies,
Little babies.
Cute, sweet, adorable babies,
Homely, sour, bratty babies.
Those are just a few.
Happy babies,
Sad babies.
Smiling, grinning, laughing babies,
Pouting, crying, screaming babies.
Infant babies, too.
Newborn babies,
Toddler babies.
Don't forget premature babies.
Last of all—best of all—
I like sleeping babies!

> — *Svetlana, grade 5*

Cookies (Grammar Poem #2)

Cookies,
Cookies,
Cookies.
Moist cookies,
Dry cookies.
Peanut butter, fudge, sugar cookies.
Banana, vanilla, strawberry cookies.
Those are just a few.
Chocolate chip cookies,
Oreo cookies,
Crunching, munching, lunching cookies.
Mixing, baking, cooling cookies.
Gingersnap cookies, too.
Fresh cookies,
Stale cookies,
Old cookies.
Don't forget store-bought cookies.
Last of all—best of all—
I like my Grandma's cookies.

— *Hillary, grade 5*

What If?

Description

This fun-to-write poem includes a "what if" question (the more preposterous, the better) and three follow-up lines that concern what would happen if the proposition were to occur. The pattern is as follows:

What if_____?
Then_____.
And_____.
And_____.
Repeat.

Lead-in Activity

Suggest a whimsical "what if?" to the students. Ask them, for example, "What if everyone in the whole world looked exactly alike?" Then discuss possible positive, negative, and/or humorous consequences to the proposition. Some responses might be "Then there would be no prejudice" or "People would not be sure who their parents were" or "Kids could fool their teachers really easily." Display a blank format of the "What If?" poem on the chalkboard or overhead and fill in three of the children's responses. Ask other thought-provoking questions, such as "What if we could talk to animals?" or "What if there were no more wars?" or "What if there was life on other planets?" Fill in the lines as they are brainstormed by various children. Then have the children ask their own "what if?" questions and, using the format provided, write their own poems. "What If?" poems are good for reinforcing the idea of cause and effect relationships.

What If? #1

What if we didn't have to go to school?
Then we wouldn't have learned how to read,
And we wouldn't know how to write,
And I wouldn't be writing this poem!
What if there were no televisions in the world?
Then we'd have to find other things to do.
And we might just play Gameboy,
And maybe we'd read more and make the teacher happy!
What if there were only one kind of food to eat?
Then we'd really get sick of it (unless it was tacos!)
And people would lose weight and get really skinny,
And Weight Watchers would go out of business!

— *Roger, grade 6*

What If? #2

What if we could talk to animals?
Then they would tell us they didn't like their food.
And they'd do what they wanted to
And soon they would be having people as pets!
What if we could be invisible?
Then we'd be able to overhear everyone's conversations,
And there would be no secrets.
And everyone would have to keep their clothes on all the time!
What if people could fly?
Then even little children could travel everywhere,
And we wouldn't need cars, and buses, and planes,
And there wouldn't be any air pollution.

— *Cindi, grade 6*

23 Tale Poems

(Adapted from A Dark, Dark Tale *by Ruth Brown)*

Description

This free-verse cumulative poem tells a "once upon a time" story using a specifically prescribed literacy scaffold. To create a complete original story poem children need only fill in certain parts of speech. The pattern is as follows:

A [*adjective, adjective*] Tale

Once upon a time there was a [*adjective, adjective noun*].
On the [*noun*] there was a [*adjective, adjective noun*].
In the [*noun*] there was a [*adjective, adjective noun*].
At the front of the [*noun*] there was a [*adjective, adjective noun*].
Behind the [*noun*] there was a [*adjective, adjective noun*].
In the [*noun*] there were some [*adjective, adjective noun/s*].
Up the [*noun*] there was a [*adjective, adjective noun*].
Across the [*noun*] there was a [*adjective, adjective noun*].
Behind the [*noun*] was a [*adjective, adjective noun*].
In the [*noun*] was a [*adjective, adjective noun*].
In the [*noun*] was a [*adjective, adjective noun*].
And in the [*noun*] there was…a [*NOUN*]!

Lead-in Activity

Read *A Dark, Dark Tale* by Ruth Brown to the children.[4] Discuss how the author uses repetition and a progressively more intense mood to build suspense. Ask the children if they were surprised by what was in the box at the end of

---

4. Ruth Brown. *A Dark, Dark Tale.* New York: Dial, 1981.

the poem. Write a group poem using Brown's format. Have the children change the title to *A Light, Light Tale* or to anything else they wish. Then have them brainstorm thirteen place nouns of their choice and demonstrate how such place nouns can be strategically arranged in the scaffold from largest to smallest to create a unique tale poem. Read the following examples:

A Sad, Sad Tale (Tale Poem #1)

Once upon a time there was a sad, sad continent.
On the continent there was a sad, sad country.
In the country was a sad, sad palace.
At the front of the palace there was a sad, sad gate.
Behind the gate there was a sad, sad porch.
On the porch there was some sad, sad furniture.
On the furniture there were some sad, sad people.
On the people were some sad, sad faces.
Behind the faces were some sad, sad secrets.
Among the secrets were some sad, sad murders.
Among the murders was a sad, sad dead man.
And in that dead man was...a HEART STILL BEATING!

— *Cristobál, grade 6*

A Bright, Bright Tale (Tale Poem #2)

Once upon a time there was a bright, bright ocean.
On the ocean there was a bright, bright sailboat.
In the sailboat was a bright, bright room.
At the front of the room was a bright, bright door.
Behind the door there was a bright, bright closet.
In the closet there were some bright, bright drawers.
In the drawers there were some bright, bright handkerchiefs.
On the handkerchiefs were some bright, bright pictures.
On the pictures were some bright, bright people.
Near the people was a bright, bright poodle.
On the poodle was a bright, bright collar.
On the collar was a bright, bright message.
On the message were the words…TAKE ME HOME!

— Chay, grade 6

24 / Fortunately/Unfortunately

Description

This free-verse good news/bad news report contains three lines of good news followed by three lines explaining why the news was not as good as it initially seemed. The first of the good news lines begins with "fortunately" while the first of the culminating lines of bad news begins with "unfortunately."

Lead-in Activity

Read children the first few pages of the story, *Fortunately*, by Remy Charlip, which is a good news/bad news story about a boy who is invited to a surprise party and on his way there encounters various fortunes that later turn out to be misfortunes: ("Fortunately one day, Ned got a letter that said, 'Please come to a surprise party.' But unfortunately the party was in Florida and he was in New York. Fortunately, a friend loaned him an airplane. Unfortunately the motor exploded…").[5] Then ask them to predict, either orally or in written form, how it will end. Older children may wish to write three more "fortunately" or "unfortunately" statements to suggest how the story will progress. Finish reading the story to children and compare their predicted adventures with the actual happenings of the boy in the story. Then ask the children to write their own "Fortunately/Unfortunately" poems.

---

5. Remy Charlip. *Fortunately*. New York: McMillan, 1980.

Whoops (Fortunately/Unfortunately Poem #1)

Fortunately, I remembered my lunch this morning.
I also remembered my homework and folded it neatly in my
   backpack.
I also made my bed perfectly without even being told.
Unfortunately, it was Saturday and I didn't have to get up.
I would have loved to have slept late because
I was tired from watching all of Arsenio last night.

— *Clarence, grade 5*

What a Waste (Fortunately/Unfortunately Poem #2)

Fortunately, we had all of my favorites for dinner:
Spaghetti, meatballs, garlic bread, and corn on the cob.
Dessert was even better—strawberry Jell-O with
   whipped cream.
Unfortunately, I had stopped at Taco Bell on the way home
   from school.
I had spent my allowance on three burritos supreme.
I was already so full I couldn't eat a thing!

— *Jennifer, grade 5*

Sounds

Description

This simple poem helps children realize the power of words by helping them to see that many words have natural sounds and actions implicit in their essence. This phenomenon is known as onomatopoeia, and children experience it firsthand when writing sounds poems that consist of an unspecified number of single-word lines.

Lead-in Activity

Define the word *onomatopoeia* for the students. Brainstorm some elements in nature; for example, thunder, hail, rain, fire, and the ocean. Take one of the elements and write it on the chalkboard or overhead in the following way: "The sound of [*noun*] is." Below this sentence stem brainstorm words that can be associated with the element and also are reminiscent of the sound of the element. Then ask the children to place the words so that the list has a poem-like quality. Brainstorm other words such as a telephone, bee, cricket, baby, bird, alarm clock, morning, that can be topics for sounds poems. Have children select one of these or another of their own creation, and write their own sounds poems. Read example poems to inspire the children. (Dictionaries and thesauruses are useful for this activity.)

Brook (Sounds Poem #1)

The sound of a brook is
Gurgle,
Ripple,
Flow,
Splash,
Lap,
Drip,
Plink,
Plunk,
Murmur,
Plunge.

— *Nicole, grade 4*

Brother (Sounds Poem #2)

The sound of a brother is
Crash,
Thud,
Brrroom,
Shout,
Yell,
Roar,
Sock,
Punch,
Thump,
Snore.

— *Raya, grade 4*

26 Too Cool

(Adapted from Earl's Too Cool for Me *by Leah Komaiko)*

Description

This is a three-line, free-verse poem that describes the
attributes of another person in the following format:

With (his/her)_____,
And (his/her)_____,
[*Name of person*] is too_____ for me.

Lead-in Activity

Read children the picture storybook, *Earl's Too Cool for
Me,* by Leah Komaiko.[6] Ask the children to share times
they were similarly intimidated by a person's seemingly
superior qualities, only to discover that the person was
approachable, and not as "perfect" as he or she first ap-
peared. Next, share the format of the poem offered in the
description section, and read aloud the following two
examples that conform to this format. As a group write a
"Too Cool" (or "too neat," or "too smart," or "too happy,"
and so on) poem on the chalkboard or overhead. Then ask
children to brainstorm some other possibilities and write a
"Too Cool" poem of their own. Have the children illustrate their poems, and place all the poems into a class

---

6. Leah Komaiko. *Earl's Too Cool for Me.* New York: HarperCollins, 1988.

book. (Remind the children that no put-downs are allowed; all poems must address "good" and "true" traits possessed by the other person, as in the examples below.)

Too Fashionable (Too Cool Poem #1)

With his Jordan Air tennis shoes
And his L.A. Gear jeans,
Randy's too fashionable for me!

— Jason, grade 5

Too Responsible (Too Cool Poem #2)

With his 5:30 a.m. paper route,
And his car-washing business on weekends,
Donny's too responsible for me!

— Brad, grade 5

27 Unknown Words

Description

This is a free-verse vocabulary-enriching nonsense poem of indeterminate length that allows children to hypothesize about words they do not know and play with the English in an enjoyable, non-threatening way.

Lead-in Activity

Define the word *hypothesis* for the children. Provide each child, or pair of children, with a dictionary. Ask each child to search for ten words (it works best to use nouns) that look and sound interesting but for which they do not know the meanings. Tell them *not* to look at the definitions. Invite them to then go around the classroom looking at the words of other children and trading words if they wish. Then have them write a poem in which they either "define" their words or use them in sentences any way they see fit. Read example poems to demonstrate the possibilities. After all the poems have been written and shared, encourage children to look up the definitions of the words in their poems to find out how close they really were! (Alliteration can also be used, as in the example poem *Laugh Until You Cry.*)

Warning (Unknown Words Poem #1)

The *gneiss* is nice to its *gnu*
So when the *scalawag* sang, I cried.
Her *foible* arrived in time for the *bootjack* to blow.
While the frog looked *connubial,*
I was really scared of his *bonhomie.*
I ran at the speed of *arthropod,*
And screamed, "Don't *cornice* me with *fibulas!*"

— *Tiffany, grade 6*

Laugh Until You Cry (Unknown Words Poem #2)

The *deuterium* dined with the dogs,
While the *dibble* was digging a *diatom.*
What a *beluga* I believe was *bellowing,*
At the guy who *gamboled* the *gland!*
The *gaffer* was given a goose
With a *cordovan* corner of cactuses.
We all laughed 'til we cried
At the *pontiff* who pickled his pie!

— *Lance, grade 6*

28 / Alphabet Madness

Description

This free-verse, eleven-line tickler (created with or without the assistance of a dictionary) can have each unrhymed line highlighting one letter of the alphabet, or each line may concentrate on a different letter of the alphabet. The following format is used:

[*Letter*] was _____.
It's [*adjective, adjective, adjective, adjective*].
[*Letter*] has a _____.
And _____.
It has seen a _____.
And a _____.
[*Letter*] [*verb, verb, verb, verb*].
And it [*verb, verb, verb, verb*].
It has _____.
[*Letter*] is always _____.
Except when it's _____.

Lead-in Activity

Group the students into pairs. Ask each pair to select a letter and make a sentence, using only words that begin with that letter (articles and auxiliary verbs excluded). Sentences may make sense, but meaning is optional! Introduce the idea of writing an entire poem in this manner using the format introduced in the description section. When children have finished their sentences, combine them in alphabetical order using the chalkboard or overhead to create a group alphabet poem. After reading the group poem chorally, read the example poems. (Point out the alliteration.) Encourage pairs of children to write their own alphabet madness poems using one letter for the entire poem or a different letter for each line. Have children illustrate their poems if they wish.

Cee Poem (Alphabet Madness Poem #1)

C was created to cause chaos!
It's cackling, cajoling, catty, and caring.
C has a cake in the coffin,
And calls the camel carefully.
It has seen a castaway in a cave,
And a cascade in a cask.
C castigates, careens, carpools, and carps.
And it cashes, carves, carries, and calms.
It has capped a canapé on a canoe.
C is always cannibalizing candles,
Except when it is covering candy.

— Rebekka & Jane, grade 6

Enn Poem (Alphabet Madness Poem #2)

N was nominated to nix needles.
It's nasty, naughty, needy, and nauseous.
N has a ne'er-do-well in the neighborhood,
And it navigates the Nile naturally.
It has seen a nanny in the north
And a nail file in a novel.
N nourishes, numbs, numbers, and nullifies,
And it nurses, nudges, notes, and nitpicks.
It has nipped a nomad on a nightshade.
N is always nicknaming nieces,
Except when it is netting nincompoops.

— Franni, grade 5

29 Wacky Week

Description

This eight-line, unrhymed poem highlights what a child has done, every day of the week, using a verb that begins with the same letter sound as that day of the week. Other words may or may not be alliterative. The poem ends with a summary statement about the whole week. The pattern is as follows:

On Sunday I [s *verb*] _____.
On Monday I [m *verb*] _____.
On Tuesday I [t *verb*] _____.
On Wednesday I [w *verb*] _____.
On Thursday I [th *verb*] _____.
On Friday I [f *verb*] _____.
On Saturday I [s *verb*] _____.
All in all, it was a very [*adjective*] week!

Lead-in Activity

Write the word *routine* on the chalkboard or overhead. Ask children if they have any kind of a weekly routine and let them describe it. You might initiate discussion by describing *your* weekly routine. Discuss: Are there certain activities that must be done on certain days? Why or why not? Tell children they will be invited to write a poem about their weekly routines—real or pretend—but each action word they use must match the beginning sound of the day of the week. These poems are based on a certain adjective that provides a theme. Dictionaries may be helpful. Read example poems to demonstrate. This is also an excellent activity to help ESL students learn verbs as well as the order of the days of the week.

An Exciting Week (Wacky Week Poem #1)

On Sunday I saw a Giant's game in Shea Stadium;
On Monday I made it to the finals in Wimbledon;
On Tuesday I took a jet to Rio de Janeiro;
On Wednesday I went on a safari in Kenya;
On Thursday I thumbed my way across America;
On Friday I found a cure for cancer;
On Saturday I sat on the beach in Acapulco;
All in all, it was a very exciting week!

— Brandon, grade 5

A Sad Week (Wacky Week Poem #2)

On Sunday I sat in a corner because I talked back;
On Monday I made many mistakes in math;
On Tuesday I tried to do better but I just couldn't;
On Wednesday I wasn't allowed to play because it rained;
On Thursday I thought I was going to throw up;
On Friday I fainted from fright;
On Saturday I slept too late and missed my game.
All in all, it was a very sad week.

— LeRoy, grade 5

30 Chores

(Adapted from Sarah Cynthia Sylvia Stout Would Not Take the Garbage Out *by Shel Silverstein)*

Description

This narrative poem suggests that there may be negative consequences for not doing household chores. The pattern for the poem requires alliteration and simple rhyme.

Lead-in Activity

Begin the discussion by asking children if they have chores to do at home. What kinds of chores? Do they have to be reminded to do their chores? What is their least favorite chore? Pair up students for a role-playing activity: one student is the child and the other child is the parent. Have children make up a scene based on a parent asking his or her child to do a chore. How does the child react and what are some excuses the child offers for not doing the chore? What will the parent do if the chore is not completed (for example, "If you don't put your dirty clothes in the hamper, you won't have any clothes to wear.")? Encourage children to share their skits.

Read *Sarah Cynthia Sylvia Stout Would Not Take the Garbage Out* by Shel Silverstein (see page 151, appendix A). Help children to identify the pattern. Ask each child to make a four-word alliteration using his or her name (fictitious, except for the first); for example, "Cathy Cassandra Candystore Clyde." Have children place their alliterated names on a piece of paper with a least favorite chore. Select a name at random and write a class poem using that name, after brainstorming three things that would happen if the chore were not done. The following scaffold will guide them:

[*Alliterated name*],
[*Neglected chore*].
[*Effect*],
[*Effect*],
[*Effect*].
[*Alliterated name*].

Gloria Greta Gardenia Gable (Chores Poem #1)

Gloria Greta Gardenia Gable,
   Wouldn't ever set the kitchen table.
   No knife or fork or plate or spoon,
   So I guess it happened pretty soon,
   That the family had to eat with their fingers!
Gloria Greta Gardenia Gable.

— Gloria, grade 5

Karen Katharine Kimberley Ked (Chores Poem #2)

Karen Katharine Kimberley Ked,
   Never had time to make her bed.
   It got to be such a terrible mess,
   And caused her mother so much grief,
   She started sleeping underneath!
Karen Katharine Kimberley Ked.

— Karen, grade 5

31

What's the Opposite...?

(Adapted from Opposites *by Richard Wilbur)*

Description

Richard Wilbur's *Opposites* is a verbal word game and provides an interesting starter for writing poetry. The poet tries to find the opposite for a word that has no opposite (see page 150, appendix A).

Lead-in Activity

Ask children to write three questions beginning with "What is the opposite...?" Have them trade their questions with other children so that no one is answering his or her own question. Have students choose two or three of their questions and answers to develop as a group, using the following literacy scaffold:

What's the opposite of _____?

_____[*word rhyming with topic*],

_____,

_____[*word rhyming with above word*].

Read the example poems. Then, as a group, brainstorm other items for which there are no opposites. Invite children to write their own "What's the Opposite?" poems with or without the literacy scaffold. Have them illustrate their poems.

Snow (What's the Opposite? Poem #1)

What's the opposite of snow?
My teacher wouldn't say so I thought *YOU* might know.
Hot water is the answer; I think it's true.
If you ski on it you'll fall right through!

— Jamal, grade 4

Bird (What's the Opposite? Poem #2)

What's the opposite of bird?
I can't think of any word
To describe a thing that does *not* tweet
And is usually *not* found on its feet.

— Nuri, grade 5

Time Capsule Poetry

Description

These poems let the students write about popular items and today's activities. By recording their ideas in free verse, this two- or three-words-per-line poetry can become an exciting and treasured experience to revisit at the end of the school year.

Lead-in Activity

Generate discussion by asking children to name the things they most like to do, their favorite foods, favorite clothing, good movies, best video game, special place, secret crush, things they would buy if they had the money, favorite recording group, and so forth. All answers should be recorded on the chalkboard. Share examples of time capsule poems. Discuss how the two- or three-words-per-line format creates a "time is flitting by" mood. Encourage children to write their own time capsules about the things that are most important to them.

Collect the poems and save them until the end of the school year. At that time, return them to the original writers. Discuss whether things have changed for them, and if so, how, since the poems were originally written. Do they still have the same best friend? Do they still want the same things? In what ways have their priorities changed?

Eleven (Time Capsule Poem #1)

Smarting off,
Acting cool,
Buying clothes,
Taco Bell,
Jurassic Park,
Good times,
Hangin' out,
Axl Rose,
Mr. Hunter's
Computer class
For sure,
Just remember,
Having fun.

— *Tasha, grade 6*

1993 (Time Capsule Poem #2)

Knicks have won,
Hurt my thumb,
Did not pass
My history class,
Designers are hot,
Punkers are not.
McDonald's is rad.
I'm never sad.
Friends are many,
Rick, Brian, and Denny.

— *Harley, grade 6*

Afterword

The power of poetry—enabling children to express their thoughts, feelings, and ideas—is, to me, nothing short of remarkable. Literacy scaffolds, as set forth in this book, make such power accessible to *all* children, regardless of their academic abilities or linguistic proficiency.

I can happily testify that poetry also has the power to change lives. Donald is a case in point. Donald was a youngster in my sixth-grade class who had academic, social, and emotional challenges. Reading at about a second-grade level and speaking (very little) with a severe stutter, he was friendless and had acquired the nickname "Sad Sack." I tried desperately to plan lessons specifically for Donald, hoping to discover some hobby or interest that would light a fire under him and elevate his status within the classroom. Nothing seemed to work.

It was about that time that I came upon literacy scaffolds as tools for helping children to write poetry. As a class, we wrote a color poem (see page 28) and then children dispersed to write their own poems. Donald was working diligently, which was totally out of character for him. He quickly penned a color poem (I know that he wrote it himself because he asked me how to spell *abandoned*). This is Donald's poem:

Green Is…

Green is the way of the sea;
Green is the green of an arrow through space;
Green is the green of a forest oak;
Green is the green of the universe;
And green is the green that abandoned the desert.

I went a bit crazy when I read Donald's poem. Previously, he had done nothing to distinguish himself. But now! We shared the poem with the principal, the librarian, four other classes, and the school nurse. Donald read his poem over the public address system and had it published in the school newspaper. He wrote many, many more poems and compiled them into a wonderful anthology. He read his collection of poems to people in nursing homes, at a talent show, and to members of the Kiwanis Club. Donald began to smile a lot and soon no one was calling him Sad Sack. For the first time in his life, he felt he had an identity—he was a poet.

Clearly, Donald's story is an unusual story; poetry will not affect all children to such a profound degree. But I am continually amazed to find that poetry writing, when properly taught, often strikes a harmonious chord in young learners, freeing them to express themselves in ways that they never before thought possible.

Every teacher can identify with my story because every teacher has at least one Donald in the class: a reticent child with untapped potential who needs a different voice with which to express him or herself.

It just might be possible that poetry writing is that voice.

Appendix A
Original Poems for Modeling

Bugs

I like bugs
Any kind of bug.
Bad bugs, mean bugs, round bugs
Green bugs, fat bugs.
A bug in a glass,
A bug on the sidewalk,
A bug in the grass
A bug in the rug.
Buggy bugs, shiny bugs,
Big bugs, black bugs.
Any kind of bug.
I like bugs.

— *Margaret Wise Brown*

(Reprinted by permission of the publisher from
*The Fish with the Deep Sea Smile: Stories and
Poems from Reading to Young Children.* Hamden,
Conn.: Linnet Books, 1988, ©1966 Roberta
Rauch.)

First Things First

A comes first, then B and C
One comes first, then two and three,
First things first.

Puppy first, and then the dog,
Tadpole first, and then the frog,
First things first.

First the seed, and then the tree,
That's the way it had to be,
First things first.

— *Leland Jacobs*

(From *Happiness Hill.* Columbus, OH: Merrill,
©1966. Reprinted by permission of R. L. Munce
Publishing.)

This Old Man

This old man
He played one
He played knick-knack
On my thumb
With a knick-knack paddywhack
Give the dog a bone
This old man came rolling home

— *Traditional*

Poem of Praise

Swift things are beautiful:
swallows and deer,
and lightning that falls
bright-veined and clear,
rivers and meteors
wind in the wheat,
the strong-withered horse,
the runner's sure feet.

And slow things are beautiful:
the closing of day,
the pause of the wave
that curves downward to spray,
the ember that crumbles,
the opening flower,
and the ox that moves on
in the quiet of power.

— *Elizabeth Coatsworth*

(Reprinted with permission of Macmillan
Publishing Company from *Poems* by Elizabeth
Coatsworth. ©1934 by Macmillan Publishing
Company, renewed 1962 by Elizabeth
Coatsworth Beston.)

The Diners in the Kitchen

Our dog Fred
Et the bread
Our dog Dash
Et the hash
Our dog Pete
Et the meat
Our dog Davy
Et the gravy
Our dog Toffee
Et the coffee
And—the worst
From the first—
Our dog Fido
Et the pie-dough.

— *James Whitcomb Riley*

Love Song for a Jellyfish

How amazed I was, when I was
    a child,
To see your life on the sand.
To see you living in your
    jelly shape,
Round and slippery and dangerous.
You seemed to have fallen
Not from the rim of the sea,
But from the galaxies.
Stranger, you delighted me. Weird
    object of
The stinging world.

— *Sandra Hochman*

(From *Earthworks*. New York: The Viking Press. ©1970 by Sandra Hochman. Reprinted by permission of Curtis Brown Ltd.)

14

What is the opposite of penny?
I'm sorry, but there isn't any
Unless you count the change,
    I guess,
Of someone who is penniless.

When people flip a penny, its
Two sides, of course, are opposites.
I'll flip one now. Go on and choose.
Which is it, heads or tails? You lose.

13

What is the opposite of doe?
The answer's buck, as you should
    know.
A buck is dough, you say? Well,
    well,
Clearly you don't know how to
    spell.
Moreover, get this through your
    head:
The current slang for dough is
    bread.

— *Richard Wilbur*

(Poems 14 and 13 from *Opposites* by Richard Wilbur. Orlando, FL: Harcourt Brace Jovanovich. ©1973 by Richard Wilbur, reprinted by permission of Harcourt Brace & Co.)

Sarah Cynthia Sylvia Stout Would Not Take the Garbage Out

Sarah Cynthia Sylvia Stout
Would not take the garbage out!
She'd scour the pots and scrape
    the pans,
Candy the yams and spice the hams,
And though her daddy would
    scream and shout,
She simply would not take the
    garbage out.
And so it piled up to the ceilings:
Coffee grounds, potato peelings,
Brown bananas, rotten peas,
Chucks of sour cottage cheese.
It filled the can, it covered the floor,
It cracked the window and blocked
    the door
With bacon rinds and chicken
    bones,
Drippy ends of ice cream cones,
Prune pits, peach pits, orange peel,
Gloppy glumps of cold oatmeal,
Pizza crusts and withered greens,
Soggy beans and tangerines,
Crusts of black burned buttered
    toast,
Gristly bits of beef roasts...
The garbage rolled on down the
    hall,
It raised the roof, it broke the wall...
Greasy napkins, cookie crumbs,
Globs of gooey bubble gum,
Cellophane from green baloney,
Rubbery, blubbery macaroni,
Peanut butter, caked and dry,
Curdled milk and crusts of pie,
Moldy melons, dried-up mustard,
Eggshells mixed with lemon custard,
Cold french fries and rancid meat,
Yellow lumps of Cream of Wheat.
At last the garbage reached so high
That finally it touched the sky.
And all the neighbors moved away,
And none of her friends would come
    to play
And finally Sarah Cynthia Stout said,
"OK, I'll take the garbage out!"
But then, of course, it was too late...
The garbage reached across the state,
From New York to the Golden Gate.
And there, in the garbage she did hate,
Poor Sarah met an awful fate,
That I cannot right now relate
Because the hour is much too late.
But children, remember Sarah Stout
And always take the garbage out!

— Shel Silverstein

(From *Where the Sidewalk Ends* by Shel Silverstein. New York: Harper & Row, ©1974. Reprinted by permission of the publisher.)

Appendix

Suggested Reading

Adults

Bator, R., comp. "Poetry." In *Signposts to Criticism of Children's Literature.* Chicago: American Library Association, 1983.

Behn, H. *Chrysalis: Concerning Children and Poetry.* New York: Harcourt Brace Jovanovich, 1968.

Bizzaro, Patrick. *Responding to Student Poems: Applications of Critical Theory.* Urbana, IL: National Council of Teachers of English, forthcoming 1994.

Boyd, G. A. *Teaching Poetry in the Elementary School.* Columbus, OH: Charles E. Merrill, 1973.

Boynton, R. W., and M. Mack. *Introduction to the Poem.* Portsmouth, NH: Boynton/Cook, 1985.

Brewton, J. E., G. Meredith, and L. Blackburn, comps. *Index to Poetry for Children and Young People, 1976-1981.* Bronx, NY: H.W. Wilson Co., 1984.

Brown, B. *Important Words: A Book for Poets and Writers.* Portsmouth, NH: Boynton/Cook, 1991.

Carey, Michael A. *Poetry Starting from Scratch: How to Teach and Write Poetry.* Urbana, IL: National Council of Teachers of English, 1989.

Chukovsky, K. *From Two to Five.* Translated and edited by M. Morton. Berkeley, CA: University of California Press, 1963.

Collom, J. *Moving Windows: Evaluating the Poetry Children Write.* New York: Teachers & Writers Collaborative, 1985.

Copeland, Jeffrey S. *Speaking of Poets: Interviews with Poets Who Write for Children and Young Adults.* Urbana, IL: National Council of Teachers of English, 1993.

Duke, C. R., and S. A. Jacobsen, eds. *Poets' Perspectives: Reading, Writing, and Teaching Poetry.* Portsmouth, NH: Boynton/Cook, 1992.

Dunning, S., M. J. Eaton., and M. Glass. *For Poets.* New York: Teachers & Writers Collaborative, 1988.

Esbenson, B. J. *A Celebration of Bees: Helping Children Write Poetry.* New York: Winston Press, 1975.

Fagin, L. *The List Poem: A Guide to Teaching & Writing Catalog Verse.* New York: Teachers & Writers Collaborative, 1991.

Gensler, K., and N. Nyhart. *The Poetry Connection: An Anthology of Contemporary Poems with Ideas to Stimulate Children's Writing.* New York: Teachers & Writers Collaborative, 1978.

Gray, S. *Teaching Poetry Today.* Portland, ME: J. Weston Walch Publishers, 1976.

Grossman, F. *Getting from Here to There: Writing and Reading Poetry.* Portsmouth, NH: Boynton/Cook, 1982.

———. *Listening to the Bells: Learning to Read Poetry by Writing Poetry.* Portsmouth, NH: Boynton/Cook, 1991.

Haviland, V., and W. J. Smith. *Children and Poetry.* Washington: Library of Congress, 1969.

Hopkins, L. B. *Let Them Be Themselves.* New York: Citation, 1969.

Hughes, T. *Poetry Is.* New York: Doubleday, 1970.

Jerome, J. *Poetry: Premeditated Art.* Boston: Houghton Mifflin, 1968.

Johnson, David M. *Word Weaving: A Creative Approach to Teaching and Writing Poetry.* Urbana, IL: National Council of Teachers of English, 1990.

Koch, K. *Rose, Where Did You Get That Red?* New York: Random House, 1974.

———. *Wishes, Lies, and Dreams: Teaching Children to Write Poetry.* New York: Random House, 1980.

Larrick, N., ed. *Somebody Turned on a Tap in These Kids.* New York: Delacorte, 1971.

Livingston, M. C. *When You Are Alone/It Keeps You Capone: An Approach to Creative Writing with Children.* New York: Atheneum, 1973.

———. *The Child as Poet: Myth or Reality?* Boston: The Horn Book, Inc., 1984.

———. *Climb into the Bell Tower: Essays on Poetry.* New York: HarperCollins, 1990.

———. *Poem-making: Ways to Begin Writing Poetry.* New York: HarperCollins, 1990.

Merriam, E. (illustrated by S. Chwast). *Finding a Poem.* New York: Atheneum, 1970.

Moore, V. *The Pleasure of Poetry with and by Children: A Handbook.* Metuchen, NJ: Scarecrow Press, 1981.

Morice, D. *How to Make Poetry Comics.* New York: Teachers & Writers Collaborative, 1982.

Nyhart, N., and K. Gensler. *The Poetry Connection: An Anthology of Contempory Poems with Ideas to Stimulate Children's Writing.* New York: Teachers & Writers Collaborative, 1978.

Padgett, R. *Pantoum.* New York: Teachers & Writers Collaborative, 1986.

————., ed. *The Teachers and Writers Handbook of Poetic Forms.* New York: Teachers & Writers Collaborative, 1987.

Painter, H. W. *Poetry and Children.* Newark, DE: International Reading Association, 1970.

Parsons, L. *Poetry, Themes & Activities: Exploring the Fun and Fantasy of Language.* Portsmouth, NH: Heinemann, 1992.

Pulsifer, S. *Children Are Poets.* Cambridge, MA: Dresser, Chapman & Grimes, 1963.

Shapiro, J., ed. *Using Literature & Poetry Affectively.* Newark, DE: International Reading Association, 1979.

Smith, J. A., and D. M. Park. *Word Music and Word Magic.* Boston: Allyn & Bacon, 1977.

Stewig, J. W. *Read to Write: Using Children's Literature as a Springboard to Writing.* New York: Hawthorne Books, 1975.

Terry, A. *Children's Poetry Preferences: A National Survey of Upper Elementary Grades.* Urbana, IL: National Council of Teachers of English, 1974.

Tsujimoto, Joseph I. *Teaching Poetry Writing to Adolescents.* Urbana, IL: National Council of Teachers of English, 1988.

Witucke, V. *Poetry in the Elementary School.* Dubuque, IA: William C. Brown Group, 1970.

Children

Adams, A. *Poetry of Earth.* New York: Scribner's, 1972.

Adoff, A. *My Black Me: A Beginning Book of Black Poetry.* New York: Dutton, 1974.

————. *Black Out Loud.* New York: Dell, 1975.

————. *Big Sister Tells Me that I'm Black.* New York: Holt, 1976.

————. *Outside, Inside Poems.* New York: Lothrop, 1981.

————. *All the Colors of the Race.* New York: Lothrop, 1982.

———. (illustrated by S. Kuzma). *Sports Pages.* New York: Harper & Row, 1986.

———. (illustrated by B. Lewin). *Greens.* New York: Lothrop, Lee & Shepard, 1988.

———., ed. *I Am the Darker Brother: An Anthology of Modern Poems by Black Americans.* New York: Collier Books, 1968.

Amon, A., adap. and illus. *The Earth Is Sore: Native Americans on Nature.* New York: Atheneum, 1981.

Arico, D. *Easter Treasures: Stories and Poems of the Season.* New York: Doubleday, 1990.

Arnold, T. *Mother Goose's Words of Wit and Wisdom.* New York: Dial, 1990.

Aylesworth, J. *The Completed Hickory Dickory Dock.* New York: Atheneum, 1990.

Baylor, B. (illustrated by R. Himmler). *The Best Town in the World.* New York: Scribner's, 1983.

Behm, H. *Trees.* New York: Henry Holt, 1992.

Bennett, J. (illustrated by S. Jenkin-Pearce). *The Animal Fair.* New York: Viking, 1990.

———. (illustrated by N. Sharratt). *People Poems.* New York: Oxford University Press, 1990.

———. comp. (illustrated by M. Roffey). *Roger Was a Razor Fish.* New York: Lothrop, Lee & Shepard, 1981.

———. comp. (illustrated by Maureen Roffey). *Days Are Where We Live.* New York: Lothrop, Lee & Shepard, 1982.

Blishen, E., comp. (illustrated by B. Wildsmith). *Oxford Book of Poetry For Children.* New York: Peter Bedrick Books, 1984.

Booth, D. (illustrated by M. Lemieux). *Voices on the Wind.* New York: Greenwillow, 1990.

———. ed. *'Til All the Stars Have Fallen: Canadian Poems for Children.* Toronto: Kids Can Press, 1989.

Brewton, S., and J. Brewton, eds. *My Tung's Tungled and Other Ridiculous Situations.* New York: Thomas Crowell, 1973.

Brown, R. *Ladybug, Ladybug.* New York: Dutton Children's Books, 1988.

Bruchac, J., and J. London (illustrated by T. Locker). *Thirteen Moons on Turtle's Back.* New York: Philomel, 1992.

Bryan, A. *All Night, All Day: A Child's First Book of African-American Spirituals.* Arranged by D. M. Thomas. New York: Atheneum, 1991.

Bunting, E. *In the Haunted House.* New York: Clarion, 1991.

Butterworth, N. *Nick Butterworth's Book of Nursery Rhymes.* New York: Viking, 1990.

Carle, E. *Animals, Animals.* New York: Philomel, 1989.

———. *Dragons, Dragons, and Other Creatures that Never Were.* New York: Putnam, 1992.

Carter, A., comp. (illustrated by R. Cartwright). *Birds, Beasts and Fishes: A Selection of Animal Poems.* New York: Macmillan, 1992.

Cassedy, S. (illustrated by M. Chessare). *Roomrimes.* New York: Crowell, 1987.

Cassedy, S., and K. Suetake, trans. (illustrated by M. Bang). *Red Dragonfly on My Shoulder.* New York: HarperCollins, 1992.

Chandra, D. (illustrated by L. Bowman). *Balloons.* New York: Farrar, Straus & Giroux, 1990.

Ciardi, J. *Doodle Soup.* Boston: Houghton Mifflin, 1985.

———. (illustrated by M. Nacht). *Mummy Took Cooking Lessons and Other Poems.* Boston: Houghton Mifflin, 1990.

———. (illustrated by E. Gorey). *The Monster Den: Or Look What Happened to My House—and to It.* Honesdale, PA: Wordsong, Boyds Mills Press, 1991.

———. (illustrated by E. Gorey). *You Know Who.* Honesdale, PA: Wordsong, Boyds Mills Press, 1991.

Clark, E. C. *I Never Saw A Purple Cow and Other Nonsense Rhymes.* Boston: Little, Brown, 1990.

Clark, A. *In My Mother's House.* New York: Viking Children's Books, 1991.

Cole, J. *A New Treasury of Children's Poetry.* New York: Doubleday, 1984.

———. *Anna Banana: 101 Jump-Rope Rhymes.* New York: Morrow, 1990.

Cole, J., and S. Calmenson. *Miss Mary Mack and Other Street Rhymes.* Long Beach, CA: Beach Tree Books, 1990.

Cole, W. *Beastly Boys and Ghostly Girls.* New York: World, 1964.

———. *Oh! What Nonsense!* New York: Viking, 1966.

Corbett, P. (illustrated by M. Maclean and C. Maclean). *The Playtime Treasury: A Collection of Playground Rhymes, Games, and Action Songs.* New York: Doubleday, 1989.

Cullum, A. *The Geranium on the Windowsill Just Died, but Teacher You Went Right On.* New York: Harlin Books, 1971.

Cummings, E. E. (illustrated by D. Calsada). *Hist Whist and Other Poems for Children.* New York: Liveright Publishing, 1983.

Dakos, K. *If You're Not Here, Please Raise Your Hand: Poems about School.* New York: Four Winds Press, 1991.

De Gerez, T. *My Song Is a Piece of Jade: Spanish/English Poetry.* Boston: Little Brown, 1984.

De Regniers, B. (illustrated by N. Doyle). *A Week In the Life of Best Friends.* New York: Atheneum, 1986.

———. (illustrated by S. Meddaugh). *The Way I Feel...Sometimes.* New York: Clarion, 1988.

———. *Sing a Song of Popcorn.* New York: Scholastic, 1991.

Dickonson, E. *Acts of Light.* Boston: Bullfinch, 1987.

———. *A Brighter Garden.* New York: Philomel, 1990.

Dunbar, P. *I Greet the Dawn.* New York: Atheneum, 1978.

Dunning, S., ed. *Reflections on a Gift of Watermelon Pickle.* New York: Lothrop, 1969.

Durrell, A., and M. Sachs. *The Big Book for Peace.* New York: Dutton Child Books, 1990.

Elledge, S. *Wider than the Sky: Poems to Grow Up With.* New York: Harper, 1990.

Esbenson, B. J. (illustrated by J. Stadler). *Words with Wrinkled Knees.* New York: Crowell, 1986.

———. (illustrated by S. Bonners). *Cold Stars and Fireflies: Poems of the Four Seasons.* New York: HarperCollins, 1991.

Espy, W. R. (illustrated by B. Cayard). *A Children's Almanac of Words at Play.* New York: Clarkson N. Potter, 1982.

Farber, N., and M. C. Livingston. *These Small Stones.* New York: Harper, 1987.

Farjeon, E. (illustrated by M. P. Jenkins). *Cats Sleep Anywhere.* New York: Lippincott, 1990.

Fleischman, P. *I Am Phoenix: Poems for Two Voices.* New York: Harper & Row, 1985.

———. *Joyful Noise: Poems for Two Voices.* New York: HarperCollins, 1992.

Foster, J. L. *Let's Celebrate: Festival Poems.* New York: Oxford University Press, 1989.

———. (illustrated by M. White and J. White). *Second Poetry Book.* Oxford, England: Oxford University Press, 1982.

Foster, J. L., comp. *A Very First Poetry Book.* Oxford, England: Oxford University Press, 1984.

Frank, J., ed. *Poems to Read to the Very Young.* New York: Random House, 1969.

Frost, R. *You Come Too.* New York: Holt, Rinehart & Winston, 1969.

———. *Birches.* New York: Holt, Rinehart & Winston, 1988.

Fufuka, K. *My Daddy Is a Cool Dude and Other Poems.* New York: Dial, 1975.

Garden, G. *The Skylighters.* New York: Oxford, 1989.

Gerrard, R. *A Pocket Full of Posies.* New York: Farrar, Straus & Giroux, 1992.

Giovanni, N. *Spin a Soft Black Song: Poems for Children.* New York: Hill & Wong, 1971.

———. *Ego Tripping and Other Poems for Young People.* Wichita, KA: Lawrence Hill, 1973.

Goldstein, B. S. *Bear in Mind: A Book of Bear Poems.* New York: Viking Child Books, 1988.

———. comp. (illustrated by J. B. Zalben). *Inner Chimes: Poems on Poetry.* New York: Wordsong/Boyds Mills Press, 1992.

Greenberg, K. *Rap.* Minneapolis: Lerner, 1988.

Greenfield, E. *Honey I Love.* New York: Crowell, 1978.

Grimes, N. *Something on My Mind.* New York: Dial, 1986.

Harrison, M., and C. Stuart-Clark. *The Oxford Book of Story Poems.* New York: Oxford University Press, 1990.

Heller, R. *Plants that Never Ever Bloom.* New York: Putnam, 1984.

———. *Merry-Go-Round: A Book About Nouns.* New York: Grosset & Dunlap, 1991.

Higginson, W. *Wind in the Long Grass: A Collection of Haiku.* New York: Simon & Schuster, 1991.

Hill, Kirkpatrick. *Tough Boy & Sister.* New York: Puffin, 1991.

Hoberman, M. A. (illustrated by C. Burstein). *Yellow Butter Purple Jelly Red Jam Black Bread.* New York: Viking Press, 1981.

———. (illustrated by B. Fraser). *A House Is a House for Me.* New York: Penguin, 1982.

————. (illustrated by M. Zeldis). *A Fine Fat Pig and Other Animals.* New York: HarperCollins, 1991.

Hopkins, L. B. (illustrated by J. O'Brien). *Circus! Circus!* New York: Knopf, 1982.

————. *Pass the Poetry, Please!* New York: Harper & Row, 1987.

————. (illustrated by H. Knight). *Happy Birthday.* New York: Simon & Schuster, 1991.

————. (illustrated by L. Molk). *On the Farm.* Boston: Little Brown, 1991.

————. comp. (illustrated by H. Stevenson). *Good Books, Good Times!* New York: Harper & Row Publishers, 1990.

Hopkins, L. B., and M. Arenstein, selectors. *Potato Chips and a Slice of Moon: Poems You'll Like.* New York: Scholastic, 1976.

Hubbell, P. (illustrated by R. Himler). *A Grass Green Gallop.* New York: Harper & Row, 1990.

Ivimey, J. W. (illustrated by V. Chess). *Three Blind Mice.* Boston: Little, Brown/Joy Street, 1990.

Jacobs, Leland, and J. Stover. *Poems for Summer.* Champaign, IL: Garrard Publishing, 1970.

Janeczko, P., ed. *The Place My Words Are Looking For: What Poets Say About and Through Their Work.* New York: Bradbury, 1991.

Johnston, T. *I'm Gonna Tell Mama I Want an Uguana.* New York: Putnam, 1980.

Jones, C. *This Old Man.* Boston: Houghton Mifflin, 1990.

Katz, M. J. (illustrated by J. Otani). *Ten Potatoes in a Pot and Other Counting Rhymes.* New York: Harper, 1990.

Kennedy, X. J. (illustrated by J. Watts). *Fresh Brats.* New York: McElderry, 1990.

Kennedy, X., and D. M. Kennedy, comp. (illustrated by J. Dyer). *Talking Like the Rain: A First Book of Poems.* New York: Little, Brown, 1992.

Koch, K., and K. Farrell. *Talking to the Sun: An Illustrated Anthology of Poems for Young People.* New York: H. Holt, 1985.

Kuskin, K. *Dogs and Dragons, Trees and Dreams.* New York: Harper, 1980.

Lamont, P. *Ring-A-Round-A-Rosy.* Boston: Little, Brown/Joy Street, 1990.

Larche, D. *Father Gander Nursery Rhymes.* Santa Barbara, CA: Advocacy Press, 1985.

Larrick, N. *Cats.* New York: Philomel, 1988.

————. *Mice Are Nice*. New York: Philomel, 1990.

————. (illustrated by C. O'Neill). *To the Moon and Back: A Collection of Poems*. New York: Delacorte, 1991.

Lear, E. (illustrated by J. Newton). *Of Pelicans and Pussycats: Poems and Limericks*. New York: Dial, 1990.

————. (illustrated by L. Brooke). *The Nonsense Poems of Edward Lear*. New York: Clarion (an Abion Book), 1991.

————. (illustrated by J. Brett). *The Owl and the Pussycat*. New York: Putnam, 1991.

————. *A Was Once An Apple Pie*. Cambridge, MA: Candlewick, 1992.

Lee, D. (illustrated by J. Wijngaard). *Jelly Belly*. New York: Bedrick, 1983.

Lester, J. *Who Am I?* New York: Dial, 1974.

Lewis, C. (illustrated by J. Fontaine). *Up in the Mountains: And Other Poems of Long Ago*. New York: HarperCollins, 1991.

Lewis, J. P. *Earth Verses and Water Rhymes*. New York: Macmillan, 1992.

————. *Two-legged, Four-legged, No-legged Rhymes*. New York: Alfred Knopf, 1992.

Livingston, M. C. *There Was a Place and Other Poems*. New York: Holiday House, 1980.

————. (illustrated by J. Spanfeller). *A Circle of Seasons*. New York: Holiday House, 1982.

————. *No Way of Knowing: Dallas Poems*. New York: Atheneum, 1982.

————. (illustrated by L. E. Fisher). *Sky Songs*. New York: Holiday House, 1984.

————. (illustrated by L. E. Fisher). *Celebrations*. New York: Holiday House, 1985.

————. *Poem-Making*. New York: Holiday House, 1985.

————. (illustrated by T. Arnold). *Worlds I Know*. New York: Atheneum, 1985.

————. (illustrated by L. E. Fisher). *Earth Songs*. New York: Holiday House, 1986.

————. (illustrated by L. E. Fisher). *Sea Songs*. New York: Holiday House, 1986.

————. *Remembering and Other Poems*. New York: McElderry, 1989.

————. (illustrated by L. E. Fisher). *Up in the Air*. New York: Holiday House, 1989.

————. (illustrated by L. Morrill). *Dog Poems*. New York: Holiday House, 1990.

————. (illustrated by A. Frasconi). *If the Owl Calls Again: A Collection of Owl Poems*. New York: McElderry, 1990.

————. (illustrated by T. LoPrete). *My Head Is Red*. New York: Holiday House, 1990.

————. (illustrated by P. Cullen-Clark). *Poems for Grandmothers*. New York: Holiday House, 1990.

Lobel, A. *The Book of Pigericks*. New York: Harper, 1983.

Longfellow, H. W. (illustrated by Ted Rand). *Paul Revere's Ride*. New York: Dutton Children's Books, 1990.

Lowe, A. M. (illustrated by S. T. Harrison). *Beasts by the Bunches*. Garden City: Doubleday, 1987.

Manguel, A. *Seasons*. New York: Doubleday, 1991.

Marcus, L. S., and A. Schwartz (illustrated by A. Schwartz). *Mother Goose's Little Misfortunes*. New York: Bradbury, 1990.

Marks, A., comp. *Ring-a-Ring O'Roses & a Ding, Dong, Bell: A Book of Nursery Rhymes*. New York: Picture Book Studio, 1991.

Martin, B., Jr. *Chicka, Chicka, Boom, Boom*. New York: Simon & Schuster, 1989.

Martin, B., Jr., and J. Archaubault. *Here Are My Hands*. New York: H. Holt, 1987.

————. *Listen to the Rain*. New York: Holt, Rinehart & Winston, 1988.

Marzollo, J. *Pretend You're a Cat*. New York: Dial, 1990.

McCord, D. *Every Time I Climb a Tree*. Boston: Little, Brown, 1967.

————. (illustrated by M. Simont). *The Star in the Pail*. Boston: Little, Brown, 1975.

————. *One at a Time: Collected Poems for the Young*. Boston: Little, Brown, 1977.

Merriam, E. *It Doesn't Always Have to Rhyme*. New York: Atheneum, 1964.

————. *Fresh Paint*. Riverside, NJ: Macmillan, 1986.

————. (illustrated by H. Wilhelm). *Blackberry Ink*. New York: Morrow, 1988.

————. (illustrated by K. Schmidt). *You Be Good and I'll Be Night*. New York: Morrow, 1988.

Michels, B., and B. White, eds. *Apples on a Stick: The Folklore of Black Children*. New York: Coward, 1993.

Milne, A. A. *Now We Are Six*. New York: Dell, 1975.

Mitchell, A. (illustrated by F. Lloyd). *Strawberry Drums*. New York: Delacorte, 1989.

Moore, L. (illustrated by M. J. Dunton). *Something New Begins*. New York: Atheneum, 1982.

Nave, Y. *Goosebumps and Butterflies*. New York: Orchard, 1990.

Nerlove, M. *If All the World Were Paper*. Nills, IL: Whitman, 1990.

Ness, E. *Amelia Mixed Up the Mustard and Other Poems*. New York: Scribner's, 1975.

Nichols, G. (illustrated by C. Binch). *Come on into My Tropical Garden: Poems for Children*. New York: Lippincott, 1988.

Noyes, A. *The Highwayman*. San Diego: Harcourt Brace Jovanovich, 1990.

O'Neill, M. *Hailstones and Halibut Bones*. New York: Doubleday, 1989.

Prelutsky, J. *It's Thanksgiving*. New York: Greenwillow, 1982.

———. *The Random House Book of Poetry for Children*. New York: Random House, 1983.

———. *Zoo Doings*. New York: Greenwillow, 1983.

———. (illustrated by J. Stevenson). *The New Kid on the Block*. New York: Greenwillow, 1984.

———. *For Laughing Out Loud*. New York: Greenwillow, 1985.

———. (illustrated by G. Williams). *Ride a Purple Pelican*. New York: Greenwillow, 1986.

———. *Tyrannosaurus Was a Beast*. New York: Greenwillow, 1988.

———. (illustrated by G. Williams). *Beneath a Blue Umbrella*. New York: Greenwillow, 1990.

———. *Poems of A. Nanny Mouse*. New York: Knopf, 1990.

———. *Something Big Has Been Here*. New York: Greenwillow, 1990.

Reeves, J. (illustrated by E. C. Clark). *Ragged Robin: Poems from A to Z*. Boston: Little, Brown, 1990.

Robertson, J. (illustrated by L. Gal). *Sea Witches*. New York: Dial, 1991.

Rossetti, C. (selected and illustrated by B. Watts). *Fly Away, Fly Away over the Sea and Other Poems for Children*. New York: North-South, 1991.

Ryder, J. (illustrated by S. Bonners). *Inside Turtle's Shell & Other Poems of the Field*. New York: Macmillan, 1985.

———. (illustrated by D. Nolan). *Step Into the Night*. New York: Four Winds Press, 1988.

———. (illustrated by D. Nolan). *Mockingbird Morning.* New York: Four Winds Press, 1989.

———. *Under Your Feet.* New York: Four Winds Press, 1990.

———. (illustrated by M. Hays). *Hello, Tree!* New York: Dutton, 1991.

Rylant, C. (illustrated by S. Gammell). *Waiting to Waltz.* New York: Bradbury, 1984.

———. (illustrated by P. Catalanotto). *Soda Jerk.* New York: Orchard, 1990.

Sandburg, C. *Rainbows Are Made.* Orlando, FL: Harcourt Brace Jovanovich, 1984.

Schwartz, A. (illustrated by S. Truesdell). *And the Green Grass Grew All Around: Folk Poetry from Everyone.* New York: HarperCollins, 1992.

Seabrooke, B. (illustrated by T. Lewin). *Judy Scuppernong.* New York: Cobblehill, 1990.

Siebert, D. *Heartland.* New York: Thomas Y. Crowell, 1989.

———. *Sierra.* New York: HarperCollins, 1991.

———. (illustrated by M. Wimmer). *Train Song.* New York: Thomas Y. Crowell, 1991.

———. *Mojave.* New York: Harper Trophy, 1992.

Silverstein, S. *A Light in the Attic.* New York: Harper, 1981.

Sneve, V. D. H. *Dancing Teepees: Poems of American Indian Youth.* New York: Holiday House, 1989.

Stevenson, R. L. (illustrated by T. Rand). *My Shadow.* New York: Putnam, 1990.

———. (illustrated by H. W. Le Mair). *A Child's Garden of Verses.* New York: Philomel, 1991.

Sutherland, Z. (illustrated by F. Jacques). *The Orchard Book of Nursery Rhymes.* New York: Orchard, 1990.

Tolkien, J. R. R. (illustrated by P. Baynes). *Bilbo's Last Song.* New York: Alfred Knopf, Dragonfly Books, 1992.

Waters, F. (illustrated by V. Julian-Ottie). *Whiskers and Paws.* New York: Crocodile, 1989.

Wayman, J. *Don't Burn Down the Birthday Cake.* Houston: Heartstone Press, 1988.

Williams, S. (illustrated by I. Beck). *Pudding and Pie: Favorite Nursery Rhymes.* New York: Oxford University Press, 1989.

Wood, A. *Silly Sally.* New York: Harcourt Brace Jovanovich, 1992.

Woolger, D. *Who Do You Think You Are? Poems About People.* New York: Oxford University Press, 1990.

Worth, V. (illustrated by N. Babbitt). *All the Small Poems.* New York: Farrar, Straus & Giroux, 1987.

Yeoman, J., and Q. Blake. *Old Mother Hubbard's Dog Dresses Up.* Boston: Houghton Mifflin, 1989.

———. *Old Mother Hubbard's Dog Learns to Play.* Boston: Houghton Mifflin, 1989.

———. *Old Mother Hubbard's Dog Needs a Doctor.* Boston: Houghton Mifflin, 1989.

———. *Old Mother Hubbard's Dog Takes up a Sport.* Boston: Houghton Mifflin, 1989.

Yolen, J. (illustrated by T. Lewin). *Bird Watch: A Book of Poetry.* New York: Philomel, 1990.

———. (illustrated by B. Degan). *Dinosaur Dances.* New York: Putnam, 1990.

Yolen, J., ed. (illustrated by international artists). *Street Rhymes around the World.* New York: Wordsong/Boyds Mills, 1992.